S.E.I.U.: Big Brother? Big Business? Big Rip Off?

By

Harriet Jackson

This book is a work of non-fiction. Names of people and places have been changed to protect their privacy.

First published by AuthorHouse 06/08/04

ISBN: 1-4184-7360-X (e-book)
ISBN: 1-4184-3939-8 (Paperback)

This book is printed on acid free paper.

DEDICATION

This book is dedicated to a man who believed in the well being of the members Of the Service Employees International Union Building Service Division in the City of Pgh., PA. He taught me well. He always encouraged me to press on no Matter what. I always remember his words "What does the contract say"? He Is my friend, my brother, and my mentor Mr. Nelson Bryant. And to a special Friend Mr. Larry F. Thomas gave me comfort in my struggle when my dear mom Was dying. He will always have a special place in my heart.

In 1980, I was hired at a local bank in the cleaning /maintenance department. The cleaning department in the bank was a closed shop, which means that you had to join the union. At the time I really did not care because I was young, happy, energetic, and was happy to have a full time job. I was in no way concerned at all about union business . It never even crossed my mind, other than I was a part of Service Employees International Union, AFL,CIO Local 29. At that time local 29 consisted mainly of building cleaners, a hand full of mechanical engineers, and a few electricians. At that time we worked directly for the building owners, which is termed 'in house'. At the bank most of my co-workers were at least 50 years old. They were kind of set back by the younger people that were getting hired, but the mindset of us (the younger people) was quite different from the mindset of the new hires of today. The president of our local at that time was Dave Glavin. I cannot comment on his performance because I had no interest in what was going on in the union realms. I was not directly involved in the way things were run, or even how they were supposed to be run. I just went along with the program for the most part. I did not question anything. To me everything was ok. I went to work on time, did my work and did it well. I was a wall washer. I actually loved my job. I must say that the senior folks there did set good examples for us. And at my worksite we had good bosses and the bank wanted that site clean and that was that. At that time we were dubbed "the cleanest 24hr building in Pittsburgh" by contractors who came in to do business. We took pride in that, even though we made very little money. But in the business world, the trend of contracting out services was becoming a reality to the cleaning industry in Pittsburgh. It was all ready being done in other states. Then it finally came to us. And on our site we had no idea what was going on.

Harriet Jackson

In 1983 the bank contracted out the maintenance services(cleaners, engineers, electricians, all union worker's services) to an outside company. That company at the time was Oliver Realty. They are now Grubb and Ellis. We had a big meeting with bank officials from the real estate department and O.R. representatives. Everyone was scared because we thought that we were going to lose our jobs, and we were afraid of big changes. Our union officials were also there and everyone assured us that everything would be the same, only we would not be bank employees anymore. We would become employees of Oliver Realty. There was no subcontractor at the time. At that time the second shift was working 3-11. O.R. quickly changed that to 10pm-6am. So that was the first change that wasn't to suppose to change!! But I still didn't care. I still had no interest in union activities. Things at our site ran just as before. Only the change in hours. But, things (were) about to change.

In the summer of 1985 there were rumors of a possible strike of the cleaners in Pittsburgh. Since I was working at night I did not get a lot of information had I been working daylight. And I must say at that time, I don't know how I would have handled the information anyway. My concerns were not with the possible strike because we worked at the bank and in the past the bank cleaners were allowed to work in past labor disputes or potential disputes because people in charge at that time. But this time it did not happen that way. We were no longer bank employees. We were O.R. employees. And when our contract was up October 31st 85,we were treated as the rest of the downtown building service workers. In the beginning of October, the talks of a strike were getting stronger and stronger. They were starting to have big meetings at the union hall. All of a sudden I started getting a little concerned. I would go to the union hall and picket signs were in the process of being made and many were already made. I went back to my worksite and told my co-workers that there is a huge possibility of a strike. I told them that it was a little more serious than we anticipated. Well, we had one union meeting before the strike. Jack Yoedt was running the show. I had no idea when he came into the picture or anything. I had no idea when he became president. All I know was that he was there. That is what happens when you don't make it a priority to be involved in your union business. At that time our site was in OBAP(Office Building Association of Pittsburgh) and it was the law firm Buchanan Ingersoll who represented the cleaning contractors who joined OBAP. So what OBAP did was they gave lists of demands and said that was how it was going to be. They refused to negotiate fairly as we all were told. They wanted big cuts in everything. Healthcare, pension, wages etc. Jack Yoedt held up the paper and said OBAP said take it or leave it. That is not bargaining in good faith. So at midnight November 11th 1985, we walked off the job and onto the streets. And that is when the most publicized strike in union history(as we were told afterwards) began. Even though several contractors have dropped out of , it OBAP is still functioning today only under a different name(moca). At that time the contractors included J.W. Galbreath & Co, Oliver Realty, Commercial Properties of Cleveland Ohio, Navro Realty ,Building Maintenance, Arnheim & Neely, Allied and Maintenance Corp. they were all in this association and Buchanan negotiated for them. When the reality finally sunk in that we were actually out on the street, it was devastating. Over half of the building service workers were older people. I mean in their 50's&60's. And it was an early and very cold winter. So we all tried to grasp this situation , got our signs, were given our picketing shifts in rotation and we got down to it. They had to bring us huge kerosene heaters. It was very, very cold. The Building Association was getting bombed by the media. I mean really bombed. How could you put the cleaning people on the streets? The senior citizens, the lowest on the totem pole? The newspaper crushed OBAP. But, they did not care. And it finally came through(from the NLRB) that it was not a strike it was a lockout because they would not negotiate with us at all. So we were able to receive unemployment. Billy Joe Jordan worked at another bank site. He was an organizer. He loved local 29. He had a heart for the people. He was a true fighter. He organized bus trips to Ohio for rallies. He was super. But most of all he was sincere. He and Keith Pipes who was the secretary treasurer at that time would come around to all the sites and get the people to sing up for benefits, and keep us posted on the progress of the lockout. And at other sites some worker, did not show up for picket duty. But no 585,668,and whatever other SEIU locals did not show up to help us, local 29 in our struggle. We had people in our local that had 32 years on the job. So I could see some of the seniors not showing up. It just was a serious health risk for them. But some did show up, and several died . over 400 members came and did their duty.

Now at some point in time the SEIU international came in and made deals (I was told) with the association that still haunt us today. The 6 hour workers was one of them. The others I am not really sure about. But for the most part we held on, we rode it out, we got unemployment and money from the strike fund. And in the end after 10 long bitter cold weeks out in the cold we came back to our buildings with a freeze. We got no increases on nothing. And personally I think that things could have been worse. I was grateful for the outcome. So were some of my co-workers. And like I said Billy Joe played a huge part in that fight. Actually he is the one who started (Justice for Janitors.) That was originated in the winter of 85 by him. It was a privilege to work with him at that time. He played a central part in that fight for the union members. I tip my hat to him. At a time when everyone was down, he kept the morale up at every site he went to. He constantly urged us not to give up the fight. They actually had scabs bussed in from other states to take our jobs. Not only was that strange, I thought that it was strange that they were mostly minorities. It was chaos at our site. The engineers thought that they would never be allow to strike because no one would be there to run the building. Well they were out in the cold with us. As a matter of fact our lead engineer Ray Harmening died leaving his picketing shift one day. That was so sad. He had a heart attack. We got a lot of sympathy in the way of newspaper adds from the steel workers, the post gazette , the port authority bus drivers, but I do not remember any other SEIU locals helping us in any manner. And now our international tells us that we have to help other locals. So in late January after everything was settled, it was time to move on.

It wasn't until after the strike that I slowly started getting involved in union affairs. I started going to the monthly meetings. As I said earlier Jack Yoedt was the president, but I am not really clear on when and why it happened. As far as Dolores Barfield was concerned, Jack chose her for his running mate because he felt he needed diversity in the office. At least that was what I was told by other members. Then she was made a business agent. The vp does not have any power. Now it was Jack and Keith Pipes (secretary-treasurer) and then Dolores. I was told that she was hired because she was a minority that could be controlled. And I will say this, she was totally incompetent. And it was as simple as that. She could not even fake it.

In 1987, I asked to be part of the negotiating team. Our contract was up in October of 88. We were negotiating with OBAP .Jack was head counsel, but he was teaching Keith how to negotiate a contract. Billy Joe was there. I do not know what capacity he was in but he was there. And there were a few other shop stewards from other buildings there also. Now, I was beginning to see how some things were done. We went back and forth with OBAP constantly. It was just tactics. They knew what they were going to do and they just took it down to the wire. 11:59. It was truly an experience for me. I will never forget it.

Our next official election for our local was in 1990. Keith Pipes was voted out and Billy Joe was voted in as secretary treasurer. Keith liked to make deals with management too much. Dick Schoenian who was the building manager at my site would talk of such dealings with Pipes. They really got along well. So it was Jack Yoedt President ,Dolores Barfield VP, Billy Joe Jordan S-T and George Detriech Recording Secretary. So that was the regime for the next 3 years. So now that I see Billy Joe in there, I start getting more and more involved. I started asking a lot of questions and reading the contract more. Bill Veatch who was an engineer on my site plus the shop steward retired. So I ran for shop steward and no one wanted it so I was it. Then several month later a guy named Dan Golibewski was hired . I was on daylight and he was on night-turn. Now at that time shop stewards did not have to pay union dues. So he wanted to be shop steward. So he got everyone to vote for him on night turn, so he officially took the position. So I went to the union office and I asked Jack could I be shop steward ondaylight (with no pay) because Danny was a very poor representative. I told him I was very interested in the union activities and I enjoyed the challenge, and I wanted to be more involved. So Jack wrote a memo that I had been appointed daylight shop steward by him. And I have been until this day.

In 1989 the bank did not renew its contract with Oliver Realty. Oxford development came in to manage the properties. The cleaners were then contracted out to Central Property Services who is a subsidiary of Oxford Development. They say they are not but they are. Now when CPS came into the picture everything started to change. See, at our site, it was our own little world. Things were not always run by the contract, but there were no problems. I really do not remember one grievance being filed at that time. So when CPS took over, they not only cut jobs they started going by contract language (when it was to their benefit) which created a ton of problems on our site. And not only that, CPS went against the contract when it benefited them!!!!!!!!

As I was attending the monthly meetings one guy really stood out. His name was Tom Kelly. He was an electrician at Carnegie Mellon University. Local 29 had a hand full of skilled workers. Tom was very intelligent, well spoken, manipulative and very thorough in his research and to top it off he had the gift of gab. Now don't forget, I am relatively new at these meetings. I soon picked up that Tom hated Jack but I did not know why. Tom always stayed on the fact that Jack never took anyone to arbitration, and he always let management have their way with grievances. He accused Jack of throwing away grievances. At one meeting Jack told tom in a round about way that if he did not like the way he did things to get another job. Needless to say Tom was stark raving mad. So at each meeting Tom was always grilling Jack . So I started getting tired of Tom. I said that Tom was picking on Jack for no reason. I would say that Jack was a good president. But he wasn't. Jack Yoedt esq. was a good administrator, but he was not a good people president. As time went on I slowly learned that. When Jack became an instructor after he left the union, he said that he was more interested in protecting the relationship with the union and management. It did not matter if the bosses were wrong, he wanted to keep that relationship no matter what. One day when I went to the union office, I asked Dolores Barfield what was up with Jack. He seemed kind of different. She told me that Jack felt out of place with the members, especially the minority members. And I still was not catching on. So then on after the meetings I would approach Jack and give him my support. I would tell him that Tom Kelly was after his job, and that was the reason he treated Jack the way he did. I fed into the trash they were feeding me. But tom Kelly was right on the money.

Harriet Jackson

I met a member at one meeting. His name is Nelson Bryant. I walked and talked with him to the bus stop after one meeting. He gained my attention. He worked at Oxford Plaza. He was a gentleman. Very smart, wise, honest, and strong. So I started to take to this man because I saw that I could learn from him. He was very mild mannered. That really grabbed me because I was much more radical than Nelson would ever be. Eventually he became my mentor, my big brother. He was so disciplined it was unreal to me. He would not say much at the meetings. He listened a lot. He spoke when he needed to. He was so wise. He was tripping me out!!!!!! I admired that. So when I would ask him questions about tom Kelly, he would tell me to go back and look at the situations in my building and compare them to what Tom was saying. Now at that time Butch Bagoon was our new business agent. He was a large man. I mean real large. Big and tall. I thought that he was a real groovy guy. He joked around a lot. But I also noticed that the grievances that were put in were never going past the first step. Butch was a terrible business agent. I learned from other members that Butch was not very good at being a business agent. Everything he did was in favor of management. Now let me remind you that I am not talking of members that want and try to abuse the fact that they belong to a union. I am talking about grievances that are filed because management has violated the contract. I personally complained to Jack, and apparently so did other shop stewards. So Jack had to let him go. Jack took over the buildings that Butch had. Of course one of the sites was the one I was at. So Jack was now our BA(business agent).. So I had submitted grievances to Jack in person. We discussed the grievances . and after that nothing was done. Now at one meeting Tom Kelly spoke of Jack literally throwing grievances in the trash. I don't know about that, but I will say whether the grievances I filed went into the trash or into a (later) box, they did not get processed. So I start thinking about what Tom Kelly said. So I went along

8

with things but I started to ask questions. I asked Billy Joe questions. I trusted Billy Joe so I would ask him questions about the way Jack was doing things. He gave me answers and he would tell me how things were, but the things that he was telling me did not seem to me to make sense about defending the contract. It made sense about defending what the (president thought) was right. Billy Joe did not want any conflict and some of the stuff he did say was correct , but I had to decipher what correct and what was not. And I had to make the ultimate decision where I was going to take a stand. Either on the right side, or the middle side. I chose the right side. That was where I wanted to be. And I found out that it is very lonely over there. At a lot of the meetings were members from the University of Pittsburgh. There was one guy I will never forget. Hazen Burton. He hated Jack Yoedt. And I was seeing all of this opposition but it just was not totally clicking yet. I would talk to Burton after meetings and he had me a bit confused. But some of the things fit into place. Pitt had a lot of problems then and still do now. Burton would say Jack does not do this and that and, I just did not know at the time what to say or think or who to trust except for one guy that stuck in my mind and that was Nelson Bryant.

One summer during the last 3 years of Jack's presidency, I joined the local 29 picnic committee. Now, Jack gave very expensive picnics. Tons of food. Invite your entire family. Lots of food games for the kids the works. You know feed the people, and they will back away. They will think more about the good picnics then they will their grievances. And when the events were over, it was business as usual. And not only did he save money on arbitrations, I understood that he invested some of the locals money well.

Election time for our officials was coming up. In the early months of 1994 I believe, there was a rumor that George Detriech was going to run for president against Jack. Now remember, George was the recording secretary. He had been for a while. When I got wind of this I was really shocked. I thought that it was a joke. Well it wasn't. Then I started to get frantic. I thought , George does not know what he is doing. There was talk at my site that the members were going to vote for George. I tried to influence the members not to go along with this farce. But most people at my site were not really satisfied with Jack. There was nothing that I could say about him to fall back on as far as defending the people. All I could say was that he was a lawyer, and he knew what he was doing. And that was nothing to work with. But I still did not think that George had a chance in hell to unseat Jack. But the University of Pittsburgh (did) want to see Jack go. Pitt has a lot of members and they controlled a lot of voting power. And at the nominations meetings, George was nominated for president. And Nelson Bryant was nominated for recording secretary. Dolores and Billy Joe stayed in place. Well, at the meeting, George came dressed in a suit and tie. He stood up accepted the nomination and vowed to demand a dollar an hour raise and arbitration for the members. Well everyone bought into it. Now the dollar an hour raise was a bit much but the vowing to uphold the contract and fight for the members was very much needed. So most people were on the Detriech bandwagon. George campaigned hard. He also had a lot of help. Tom Kelly was from CMU and Hazen Burton was from Pitt. Not many people were on Jack's side. And Jack did not even bother to campaign. All I remember was 4 by 7 cards that had a couple lines about his contract negotiation capabilities. Well, needless to say it failed. Jack lost miserably. It was a landslide. Jack was kind of arrogant and he did not put very much into his campaign. George had vans picking up people from the universities to come to the union hall to vote for him. When it came time for Jack to turn over the leadership to George, he did it gracefully. Everyone in the union hall was very happy. Especially Tom Kelly. After the vote when I went outside, Jack was standing outside against the wall with his hands in his pocket with tears in his eyes. I believe he was truly stunned. I gave him a hug and he pushed me away and walked away. I was a little set back by that but there was nothing to say. From what I understood from Billy Joe, when an officer gets voted out he receives a large sum of money. Severance pay I believe. Anyway, they get large sums of money and it is not pension money. So now it was Jack out and George in.

George did not have a very good personality. In fact he was a very nasty person. That on top of not knowing what you are doing can be very bad in some circumstances. George hired two new business agents. I really do not remember their names. Well no, one's name was Gary Hall. He was a security guard from Gateway Center and the other one was named Jim I believe. Jim was the agent for my site, and Gary was to supposed to have numerous degrees from some universities? George hated Dolores. He wanted to get rid of her in the worst way. She was useless and he did not want her around. But he could not do it because she was an elected official. Now, he wanted to get rid of Billy Joe too, but he would have had a riot on his hands. Billy Joe is a tough man and George had no other recourse than to respect him. Billy (made) him respect him. When George took over, everything started going by the bylaws. He was so ridiculous that the bylaws book was thrown at him by the executive board members. George wanted to do what he wanted but he was held to the bylaws. And he did not have the knowledge that Jack did so he was basically alone. I was so upset at him winning that I called the international and told him that our local was in trouble. But George had done nothing wrong (yet). He talked to Delores like a dog and she took it. He frustrated the secretaries so, so bad. The only ones that did not really have a personality problem with George were Nelson and Billy. And frankly I really did not have any sympathy for Delores cause she should have stood up for herself. She was a pathological liar and a horrible business agent, and George just crushed her and she kept her mouth shut because she had no recourse. If it had not been for Billy getting George up off Delores's back he probably would have run her out of there. But that is just my opinion. Jack had left the local in pretty good shape money wise. As I understood it he invested a lot of the local's money in mutual funds. So George had a little cushion to work with. But he started going hog wild with the money. Now Jack did not leave millions. Every case does not need to be arbitrated. If George's personality had been better, he could have had a lot more support. So the help and advice he could have gotten he did not because he was so difficult to work with. So in the long run, the members suffered. His chosen business agents did not have a clue. And they did not want to take any advice from Billy or anyone else. Now in our up coming contract negotiations (1995) people were a little uneasy. I know I was. Everyone knew that George did not know how to negotiate a contract. He knew it too. So what he did was he had the law firm we retained (Joe Pass &Company) do all of the negotiating. It was very costly and we ended up in the red. Very quickly I might add. During the negotiations that members were not a part of, the feedback was not very good as far as the members were concerned. One of the lawyers named Ernie from the law firm was our negotiator. Now SEIU was still dealing with OBAP and Central Properties was separate. I remember the OBAP buildings getting a bad deal on vacations and some other things that George allowed in the contract, but the Central Properties buildings got a bit of a break on some things. We had a meeting at the union hall for an explanation of the things that the members did not agree to and no one could give us any straight answers. We could not get any answers from anyone. Not Ernie, George, Billy, or Delores. So many calls and letters went to the international, that they (had) to respond. And the only reason why they responded was because of the finances. It had nothing to do with the well being of the members. So the international came in and had this huge meeting at the Doubletree Hotel. Everyone testified against George even Tom Hoffman who was put in charge as an overseer of the local when we voted down a merger and trusteeship. I was curious as to where this Tom Hoffman came from. Billy said he was with local 585. That was it. So now he is our overseer. The fact that a lawsuit was going to be taken against the local also got the international's attention. George illegally reopened the contract and took out some organizing language. It was crazy. At the next monthly meeting, George got up to give his report. As usual everyone left the meeting goofy because George talks in riddles and he lies. I might add this, when George would talk there would always be this little ball of spit on his bottom lip that he would suck in and out as he talked. To this day that truly puzzles me. Never mind why he would do it, (how did he do it!!) I have never seen anything like it. Not only was it gross it was more....strange (to me). And everyone made jokes about the fact that he wore a toupee. Well one thing I can say is that his hair was always in place. The toupee did not bother me, it was that ball of spit!!!!! You had to see it!!! I must say that some of George's intentions were good. I really believe he wanted to help the members fight for what was right. The employers would make fun of him to members and that was a little embarrassing , but him being in office brought a lot of things out as far as operating procedures that were not being done in the previous administration. From what I was told and what I had seen , Jack was taking things into his own hands instead of going through the board. Hermaine Delaney made light of that. She was working at Duquesne University at the time. Everything that was wrong in Jack's administration came out in this one because George was totally inept. Not only that he had no one to carry him. And he had no one to carry him because no one liked him. He (made) people not like him. But him coming into the office attempting to do things Jack would not do and actually doing things that Jack would not do, opened up the door for the members. And even though Tom Kelly pushed for George, he tried to stand behind George and encourage the members but it just was not working. And Tom Hoffman, I never really did understand his position. I was told that he first came from the international. You can work for the international and be paid by them. If a local sees fit to hire you then you will get paid by that local. Now before the meetings with the international, Tom Hoffman worked out of the local 29 office. I asked Billy what exactly was Tom. He said Tom was looking for a stable position within a local. He wasn't really doing anything. And Billy said "he makes 50,000 dollars a year". And Billy said at the private hearings with the international with George, Tom testified against George. Billy got a kick out of that cause he said George's hair on his neck stood up. But check this out, at one general membership meeting, Hermaine Delaney who worked at Duquesne University stood up to let the fact be known that a co-worker named Julius was spreading the rumor that the accusations against George were unmerited and it was a "black thing". And she was very upset about that. I asked her why would he say that and she told me that she understood that the strategy came from Tom Hoffman to try and lessen the pressure on George. Well, when it came time to have the good and welfare of the meeting, I stood up to call Julius to the floor and he had snuck out of the meeting!!!! So I was starting to see how Tom Hoffman actually was. I was told that he did this to create dissention among the black and white workers. Do I believe it? Yes . Towards the end of Georges reign I think he knew that he was not going to get re-elected. I think everyone knew that. In the early months of 1997, Billy Joe Jordan started to campaign for president. He was approached by numerous people to run including myself. He was going to do it. I also found out that Nelson Bryant was going to run for secretary treasurer. Now the recording secretary position was going to be open. I told Billy that I was interested in running for it. He seemed a little disappointed and said that he was hoping that

14

Evelina from CMU would run for it. Well, I approached Evey. And I said to her that if she wanted it that I would run cause I trusted her. Instead she told me no. She said that she would back off if I was going to run. Of course Nelson was my encourager. So I was nominated. And I was automatically the new recording secretary because no one challenged me. The job required a lot of writing, speaking in front of the membership, and attending every meeting taking the minutes. Well, I had no problem with any of that. And I distinctly remember after the meeting for the nominations, Tom Kelly approached me and said "how does it feel to have a job that no one else wants"? He then followed by saying "I'm just kidding". He really was trying to get back at me for not supporting George and not giving him undue respect that he thought he deserved from a (certain group of people.) He seemed to have the attitude that he was a lot more educated than other people. Tom also ran for trustee and won.

I would frequently go down to the union office to see Billy and talk about what was going on. I had a good relationship with the secretaries, Irene the senior secretary and Kathy Durkin. They knew that I was going to be the new recording secretary so they showed me where my files would be kept in the office and they showed me my mailbox. I may add that George had bulletproof glass put up and locks put on the doors because a member that he said something very ,very rude and unnecessary to threatened to do him bodily harm. Whoever it was apparently was not kidding for George to go to those extra measures!!!!! I never found out who it was. Anyway I was very excited about Billy running for president. I was also very excited about Nelson running for sec-treasurer. But what threw me for a loop was that no one and I mean no one in that office wanted Nelson in the office. Not one person. Everyone spoke against him. The secretaries talked of how terrible his minutes were. No one wanted him in the office except for me. And don't forget Tom Hoffman is still stationed at the local 29 office(literally taking up office space). Now the reaction to Nelson coming to the office still shook me. So I had to go back and regroup. Certain conversations I had with certain officials started to come back to me. Delores stayed stuck up under Billy because he carried her. Diane Topakian from the state council said Dolores was "totally useless". And she (Dolores) had the nerve to not want Nelson in the office. Anyway I started to talk to Nelson about the atmosphere in the office. I felt he needed to know so that he would know what was going on. Well, the elections went as expected. Billy had folks bussed in from anywhere members had to be picked up. Billy beat George without a sweat. Nelson won , Dolores won, I was already in, Tom Kelly and Hermaine Delaney were the trustees. Hermaine retained her position. And Rich Johnston was the new board member. So at the May membership meeting Tom, Rich and myself were sworn in. Now, here starts the time when I was directly involved in the union business. So I am much clearer on times and dates. I actually started my recording secretary job on June second 1997. I was pumped, but somewhat nervous. Like I said I had to be at (every) meeting Local 29 had. I had to take the notes and report it back to the members. I was really loving this. I really wanted to be involved with the people and I was. I was nervous reading in front of the people at first, but I got use to it. I loved being on the board helping to make decisions to help our members. Now at this time me and Hermaine really did not get along. I had decided to tape the executive board meetings and some of the general membership meetings, then take most of my notes from the tapes. I introduced the idea at the ex-board meeting, and it went over well. So I did tape some meetings. The general membership meetings were harder to tape because I was on the stage and the people sitting out off the stage was a little hard to pick up. The executive board members were paid 75.00 a month. I was paid 25.00 dollars more because of what my job involved. No one liked writing and speaking. I loved the writing

16

part. The speaking part, I had to get use to. And I did not have self restraint. I had a big mouth and no restraint. Nelson would tell me to calm down. His calmness I admired so, so, much. At all the board meetings Hermaine was very nasty and rude. She was a very good shop steward and board member, but she was very nasty. She had a very nasty personality. I would see her on the street and speak to her, and she would not speak back. So I quit speaking. But she was very smart and I learned from her. She was in this long before I was. She would be up at the meeting telling the officials off, and telling Dolores how inept she was. And she would always tell the officials that she worked for Duquesne University and not the local. So at he executive board meetings, I am learning what is going on behind closed doors. Well, we had a lot of cleaning up to do from George 's administration. The first thing we had to do was outline a budget. We did not come into one. So we had to get that in place plus deal with the members. All of the top officials were also business agents. First we owed our attorneys (Joe Pass & Company) 36,000 dollars. Joe Pass was with Local 29 for a long time. Plus he was with the ATU Local 85, the Port Authority bus drivers. I always heard his name, but I had never met him until we had problems with the contract George messed up. Well when I met him in person, I was a bit honored. I shook his hand and told it was a pleasure to meet him and that the press did him no justice!!!! He is a good looking man. And I told him that. Well, that September after the elections at the Labor Day Parade, I was walking around from place to place. As I was mingling I heard a guy talking about the people to get good representation from. This guy was from CMU. This guy said to the other guy, get in touch with Nelson Bryant. He is straight up he stands for the members and he don't play no games and you can trust him. He also told the guy that he had never personally met Nelson. That says a lot for a person's integrity. Nelson was everything that the guy said he was. So it was clear that Nelson stood out above all of them in that office. That is why he was not liked in the office. And he was not liked at all by the management bosses. But they respected him. They had to. He was straight up he did not play with those employers. He did not make deals with them. He was straight by the book. I learned so much from him.

Billy Joe was a good people president but he was not a good administrator. Even though I feel that he really did not want me in the office either, I still loved him. He was a good friend. And still is. But I was seeing that he was a little difficult to work with. He is a very strong man with a very broad ego. That was hard to deal with. We got into arguments and I would not back down and neither would he. At times he did not like to be questioned. Well, everyone has to be questioned at some point. Now we were trying to get our budget together. And at the same time we were getting a lot of flack from a (certain group) of members because our administration was all black…and yes that does make a difference. And Tom Kelly would try his best to give our top officials a very hard time at the executive board meetings. Tom would get under Billy's skin like he did mine. At a certain point Tom just stopped talking to me. I didn't care. Now, he tried to break Nelson and he could not do it. That frustrated Tom to the max. Billy was not wrong a lot of times but Tom just questioned him to upset him. I will say that I enjoyed working under Billy. He introduced me to the inside of union world. He really wanted me to learn. And he also got other lay members to get involved in the union world. I went to conventions, conferences and seminars. I was just exposed to so much and it was all because of Billy Joe. When we would go out of town, I would always ask him if I could have a private room. He did it. I will say again I learned a lot because of him. And I truly thank him for that. And him involving lay members encouraged them and us to want to move up and run for office some day. He encouraged that. He believed in that. And I respect him for that. Now at these conferences, I was beginning to see that something was wrong.

We were at these conferences with Rosemary Trump and Local 585 people. Local 585 was mainly health care. Well we were barely recognized. We were dissed as the young folks say. Now there was always the rumor that Rosemary wanted Local 29. Now that was how it was told to me by numerous people, including Hermaine Delaney, Billy Joe, Catherine Brown(a retiree) and general members. Even though Local 585 had mostly health care workers, they did have some building service workers, but they were very few. Mostly in the suburbs. They also had health care workers in many different areas. Even West Virginia. They were spread out. It was not consolidated like we were in downtown Pittsburgh. It was apparent that where Rosemary could get members she did. I will say she built a large dues paying structure. She had over 12,000 members as I was told. Our setup was totally different. Their dues payments were different from ours. Local 585 had a lot of part time workers. So their dues were structured to the amount of money they made. On a percentage scale. Ours was the same across the board. Now back to these conferences, I was starting to be really dismayed. Building services was never really recognized. Even though we were really out numbered by the healthcare workers we were all under the service umbrella. We were all SEIU. But building services was not acknowledged much at these conferences. It reminded me of the way the employers treat us. They treat us like we are nothing because of the service we perform. And to me that is how we were being treated at these conferences. So I sat back and I listened. When we went to these conferences I was right with my mentor Nelson Bryant. He was like a brother/father to me. He saw the discouragement in me because of what I was seeing, yet he continued to encourage me and press me to go on. This was all new to me and he saw that I was not handling it well. And his encouragement was most sincere. I was seeing why Nelson really had no one in his corner (other than me). When you stand for what is right and you attempt to do the right thing, a lot of times you do not have a huge backing. Nelson told me that his office was being sabotaged. And Nelson is not a liar. Nelson had a computer and he had stored a lot of his business agent work on his computer. Well somehow all of his information was erased. Now not anyone is able to do that. You have to know what you are doing. Now Billy did not know squat about computers. As a matter of fact he hated them. Dolores, she did not know much either. I'll leave it at that. Now Cathy knew a lot about computers and so did Tom Hoffman who was still at the local 29 office. You have to know how to go into a hard drive and erase the stored files. Billy told me he continued to hound the international to remove Tom from the office because we needed the office space. He was of no use to us. And Billy always told me that he was sneaky. But after the Julius incident, I could see that for myself. And one day Billy Joe said he makes 50,000 dollars a year. He was paid. Paid for doing nothing. But I could not understand why it was so hard to get him out of our office. Billy had to explain to me that Tom needed a stable local to work from. I guess you could say that he worked for and was paid by the SEIU international or the state council. When you work for the international or state council, or the different regional offices, that is who pays you. I understand that Tom was looking for a position with a SEIU local so he would not have to travel from place to place. He wanted to be stable. Well he was finally sent to 585, so he was out of our office. The computers that were in the office were old, except for Cathy's. As far as I know Tom had his own set-up. Cathy had to have the good stuff because she was the secretary. But I remember at one executive board meeting I strongly suggested that we get another new computer and get online. Billy was totally against it. So I asked the board members, and Hermaine said "well I don't know nothing about computers so I don't know if we need one or not". I will say this in all honesty Hermaine stuck up under Billy like I did Nelson. But she stayed under Billy cause not only were some their thoughts the same, she could manipulate him to a certain degree. She could not do that with Nelson. So I argued fervently that we needed to be online. The international was on every president about organizing. I tried to tell Billy we needed to be on line. But he was very adamant about not getting a new computer system that would be online. That was part of the ego situation I was referring to. Whether you like computers or not, you cannot successfully run an organization/business without being connected to the internet. It's as simple as that. I believed that we were all supposed to be trying to make our local productive. But when one part of the body refuses to even try and learn from the other, then you will have problems. Billy was hard to work with at times.

I thought surely that when Nelson came into the office that he would be given all of the Central Property Services buildings. I started to get happy. Well I wasn't happy for long. Vice president Barfield continued to be our business agent. That was another problem I had to continue to deal with. She was as useless as tits on a bull. There is just no other way to put it. Well at some point there was an arbitration meeting for a grievance I had filed with a co-worker. Now, I asked Dolores wasn't I supposed to be there. She said no. When I told my co-worker Niki that I could not be there she was a scared. Well, when she came back from that meeting, she was crying and could hardly talk. I asked her what had happened. She said that when they asked Dolores for the papers with all the information on them, Dolores said that she did not have them and she did not know all the details, and that I had all the information. Well needless to say I was stark raving mad. I went to the office after work to see Billy. I called him first to make sure he was there. When I got there Dolores was there and I told Billy that she had no business being a business agent, she did not know what she was doing and that she needs to step aside. I was very loud and I was very upset. And after I got done yelling at Billy, she said, that she did not know that I was supposed to be there. Now she had been a business agent for ten years, and she claims that she did not know that. Now I saw firsthand why Hermaine would crush her at union meetings. The only reason that she was able to stay vp was because no one that was well known in the local ran against her. And needless to say, that case was lost, because of Dolores Barfield. And she had the nerve to feel bad. And then her habitual lying was another thing I had to deal with. That is so hard. You have to try and decipher what is true and what ain't. I am telling you, dealing with a pathological liar can wear you down. My boss the director of operations is a pathological liar. Being lied (to) is one thing , being lied(at) is another. Now we had a few other board members, Rich Johnston, Walter Moorefield, Cal Moran and Dolores Mccoy. They really did not have much to say most of the time. Tom Kelly would try his best to twist everything Nelson did and said. Everything Tom threw at Nelson, Nelson backed it up with facts and put it right back in Tom's lap. Tom would be so frustrated . I once made the remark to him that he things all black folks are stupid. Now that was when he flew off the handle. Of course he said that was a misjudgment of his character. And I told him no it wasn't. After that he did not have much to say to me. I think he was a good board member. He would keep you on your toes. But I will say it was so beautiful to just watch Tom try to play word games on Nelson and try and manipulate him and Nelson would calmly listen to everything Tom would say, then answer the question with a question that Tom could not answer. I admired Nelson's tact. I had none. He would often remind me of that. Billy once referred to Tom Kelly as being like the late Rev Jim Jones. Well when Tom brought that up at the membership meeting, I almost lost it. Tom sounded like he was going to cry. He said in no way was he like Jim Jones.

Later on I found out that decisions were being made in the office without Nelson being aware of them until after the fact. Nelson was on the outside. That troubled me because not only was it not right it was bad for the administration. Nelson was very troubled by this. He was second in command and he should have been included in everything. I know he was frustrated and I did suggest to him that he approach Billy about it. Nelson stood up for the members. He was all for the members. He was for what was right. And he was revered by management. But as I was seeing things everyone was not in favor him. Jealousy played a huge role. Anyway Nelson did not approach Billy right away. And I must say that Billy not including Nelson ,and not informing Nelson was totally wrong. Nelson was also very hurt by all of this. His office and computer was being sabotaged, someone actually killed his plants. He had plants in his office. And of course no one knew nothing. But one thing I will say, even though Nelson was treated as he was by his own co-workers, as a whole the members that had come in contact with him directly and those that did not have direct contact with him and only knew of him, highly respected him. His integrity was impeccable. He was trusted because the members knew what he was about.

In, I believe early 1998, Nelson had a slight physical setback. He was off for several weeks. I sure missed him at the meetings. He would ride me home from the meetings. Now I had to ride home with Billy and Hermaine. I did not mind Billy, but Hermaine could not stand me. One night me and Hermaine was out in the parking lot arguing about who was going to sit in the front of the car. I was just being silly about the whole thing. I thought it was funny. She was very upset. When Billy came to the car, he just stood there and looked up in the sky. He asked me to get in the back and I said (happily) ok!!!!!!!!! The university of Pittsburgh was one of Nelson's sites, so Billy took it over when Nelson went on sick leave. Now Pitt has 300 plus members and apparently that means voting power. There are some many different classifications out at Pitt and it I think that had some things to do with their problems. Pitt always had a lot of problems.

Being the business agent out there was a very formidable task. Well, Pitt was not satisfied with the representation they were getting from Billy and Nelson. Nelson got a little flack but Billy got a lot. And a lot of the letters that were written to the international (and there were a lot) about Billy. And a lot of them were lies. They came mostly from a certain group of people. They actually said that he was stealing money. We were getting out of debt. So what money was being stolen? And not only that we were really getting pressured to put an organizing plan into place. So that was really number one on the list as far as the international was concerned. But local was still member oriented. So Billy introduced the fact that he had to hire an organizer. But we could only afford a part time organizer. So Billy had to find an organizer.

At the next executive board meeting Billy had his new organizer, John Listisen. I don't really know how Billy chose John, or came up with his name. As a matter of fact I never asked him that. Billy said that he was a loud mouth bar room guy that talked tough. Billy said that he thought that he would fit the job well. John worked at the Pittsburgh post-gazette for over ten years I believe. He worked the 4-12 shift cleaning. He was a local 29 member. He told us at the executive board meeting that his boss would allow him to do organizing work on company time for a few hours. Now I was pretty surprised at that (and so was everyone else) but I did not question him about it. Some of us members did question that among ourselves. John was very polite when he came to speak to the executive board. He gave us a rough layout of what his duties would be. He told us that he would be going to the nonunion buildings and organizing (attempting) the members. He would make a report and give it to the board monthly. And to the membership meeting monthly. (And just for the record, the international told Billy that we had to get a new computer that would be online. John needed it for his job. Plus we needed it period. But for Billy he would not take my advice ,he had to get a command from the international. Needless to say we had a new computer within a week or so.) John would do his job and have to make a report to give to the members. That is what I loved about local 29 we were member oriented. We worked for the people and we reported back to the people. We had to. We were supposed to. That is the way it should be. When John was introduced at the general membership meeting, he was a whole different person. He was very brash, condescending and down right rude. He jumped all over the Pitt members about how they did not come out to rally. Well, at the membership meetings, there were very few Pitt members there. And he also continued to get on the downtown members too. At that time Hermaine was still working at Duquesne University. Duquesne was also in house and they made more than the downtown buildings. Hermaine made sure that everyone knew that too. She would brag about it from time to time. But she jumped all over John for putting the members down. She would light into him. She would tell him that people are tired and did not always feel like rallying. I mean she let him have it. And that he had no right to come in here trying to make people feel bad. And he did and he continued to do it. He always made reference to the fact that he made 14-15 dollars an hour and that he really did not need this organizing job, and that local 29 could not afford to match his wages. I guess that (you could guess) that no one really liked him. He started off on a bad foot. I think Billy had to calm him down a bit. But he for the most part, he continued his ways. By his reports, John seemed to be doing a good job. And he did say that he liked it. But still there were a lot of complaints from a select group at the university of Pittsburgh about Billy Joe. So, at one point when things seemed to be picking up for us, they would be shot down. For instance, Children's Hospital of Pittsburgh was nonunion. John went there to attempt to organize them. He got signed cards from the employees to join local 29. When John made that announcement at the membership meeting everyone was really happy. Then later, it came from the international that we (local 29) could not take Children's Hospital because we were stepping into the healthcare division. Now I don't know if SEIU 1199p got Children's at that time or 585. John did not say which SEIU local complained. I am inclined to think it was 1199p. But if 585 can get cleaners, why were we rejected from organizing healthcare workers? And why was Children's not a part of the SEIU healthcare before this? John was very upset and so was the membership. But I really don't think they realized the statement that was being made here by the international. At that particular time I did not really know either. As time went on, it became clear that SEIU international did not want Local 29 to be successful. When Nelson returned , he took a little while to settle in and get back into the groove. And when he did, he said at the board meeting that he wanted to know everything that went on in the office. He claimed his position as second in command and he wanted to be in on everything that happened and every decision being made. Needless to say that did not sit well with Billy.

In late 1998 I saw a member from the Liberty Center Building, and she said that she heard that we were going to merge with local 585. Well, it through really threw me for a loop. Plus I got a little scared. At this point I was totally stunned at the rumor because me being on the board, I had heard nothing of the sort. So I asked around and I was told that Rosemary Trump who was the president of 585 had always had her eye on local 29. So I dismissed the rumor. But it was still always in the back of my mind. And I also wondered if so why now? But as the months went by Billy was talking of a merger with local 585. Soon it became common knowledge that President Andy Stern wanted us to merge with local 585. Things were just starting to get better for our local. We had paid off attorney Pass which was a huge bill, and we were focusing more on organizing and we were handling the grievances and I just could not understand why. Everything was coming together for our local and the merger thing just seemed to come out of the blue to me. But apparently this had been in the making for a while. Everyone I talked to in the office, seemed to be on edge. Even Cathy the secretary. She was making over 30,000 a year. The executive board fought with Billy about the raise that her and Irene had just got but Billy wanted them to get it. We were struggling to pay of George's mess and all Cathy wanted was a raise. She had a cake job. And when she found out that the board did not want to give them a raise, she started giving us our board checks whenever she wanted to. Irene wasn't so bad. She was getting ready to retire, but Cathy was upset at the time. She most certainly had a lot of nerve. She could play Billy's feelings and she did. She still has an attitude with me today, but I don't care. But back to the merger, at one executive board meeting Billy announced that Andy Stern wanted us to merge. So when I talked with Billy personally, I told him my feelings from the beginning....no. And I said that I would encourage no one to accept this merger. And I told him all we had to say was no. Then he told me that it was not that "cut and dry". So at the executive board meeting, we all decided that Rosemary should come in here and talk to us. And one thing that kind of threw me for a loop was Tom Kelly's reaction. It took a while but I was starting to notice that there was a lot more going on here than what I knew. Billy was not happy with this merger yet he was backing it. So that led me to believe that something was very wrong. Or wrong in my eyes. No one knew what was going on. I was trying to understand why after George's administration that the international would so fervently want us to merge , so you have to look at the situation. An all black administration and lots of complaints. Well, I guess that's enough!!!!!!!!!!!!!!! A perfect and (easy) way to take a local and merge it with another. (Now), at the membership meetings, the merger was the top priority of discussion. Billy had to speak on it. I would listen to what he had to say then I would think about it. He said at the meeting that the international said that the members of local 29 were unable to make proper leadership decisions. Yes, when a president was not up to what the members thought in the way of honoring the contract, he was voted out. We controlled our voting power. I believe that if Jack Yoedt had fought legitimate grievances, along with his overall knowledge, he would still be president. I learned a lot from him. So, even though the international basically said that the members of local 29 were stupid, Billy was backing them. That truly troubled me. I was fourth in order to give my report at the membership meetings. So when it was my turn, I was very upset and I let Billy have it. I blasted him right at that meeting in front of the people. I asked him how could he let Andy Stern call us stupid like that? And then agree with him? I told the people no. I was in no way in favor of a merger. I yelled that Rosemary just wanted our union dues. That she was in no way concerned about our wants and needs. Now from where I was at ,I was pinning everything on Rosemary. I always heard the rumors that (she) always wanted our local. So my focus really was Rose. So I strongly told the people that we should not want a merger. I was very upset that morning. So the meeting ended and we would get back to the members after we had Rosemary come and meet with the executive board.

Before the special executive board meeting, I would talk to Billy about the merger. He was not happy about it. He told me that he went to see Andy Stern to talk with him and that Andy showed him a stack of complaints against him. But he said that the complaints had no weight on the decision to merge. I believe it had a lot to do with the decision to merger. Not only was Billy not happy about the merger, he was very sad. It hurt him deeply that the local was being taken from him. And that is exactly what was happening. There was sadness in his voice. At least I noticed it. But when he got in front of the membership, he acted as if he was all for it. All that was being said was that we better merge. Better. Well, March of 99 we finally got a meeting with Rose Trump, Emily Young from the international whom I was told was an attorney, and John Ronches a person from the SEIU Eastern Region. What his title was I really did not know. So before the meeting got under way, I was walking around the union office talking with the officers. You could have cut the tension with a knife. Or maybe it was not tension, it was more like fear. I told Nelson that I was not voting in favor of the merger. Nelson said it did not matter because if the executive board did not approve it, they (the international) were going to (take it from us). He said that was what John Ronches was walking around the union office saying. So I asked Billy if this guy was trying to scare us, and Billy said no. So I asked why he was walking around with this attitude. No answer. Everyone was so nervous. Tom Kelly was the last one to show up. The meeting finally started. Everyone introduced themselves. John Ronches started off by telling us why we had to merge. He went on to say how he was very concerned about the future of local 29 and that he wanted the best for us. I said to him that he was not concerned about us ,local 29. I told him that he was (sent) here to do a job, and that job was to convince the executive board to agree to a merger as soon as possible, so don't act like you came here to do us a favor. When I said what I said, I did not yell nor was I rude. I was confident. I said what everyone else wanted to say. Much to my surprise, this man almost fell apart! His entire attitude changed. He went from tough guy to Mr. wimp. I was shook up!!!!! He said that I insulted him. Now remember I have never met this man before in my life. You would have thought I cursed the man out and called him all kinds of names. It really threw me for a loop. He went on to say that I did not like him(???????) Like I said I never met the man before in my life. His reaction truly floored me. The fact that he came here throwing his weight around, having everyone in the office scared, was what set me off. And the "I care about local 29" well, I just did not want to hear any lies. And all this time Rose was looking for a business agent for the soon to be division 29 local 585. She had her eyes on Hermaine. Anyway they went on to tell us about how the merger would help us financially, and how more members would scare the employer into giving us what we wanted at contract time, and the main thing was we had to start a serious organizing campaign. They said that we were not able to do that at this time because we did not have the funds. But if we merged then we would have the funds because local 585 had the resources. He told us we were virtually bankrupt. They went on to tell us that the downtown building contract was up in several months. We were told by Rose ,John and Emily that if we did not merge with local 585,and if we went on strike that coming November, that (no) SEIU local would step in to help us and the international would not help us. We would be on our own. Now we pay quite a bit of money in per capita taxes. Hundreds of thousands of dollars. The SEIU international makes sure that they get their tax money. Let me make it clear that Billy Joe was one of the lowest paid local presidents in the SEIU. Billy was in the mid 40's, I was told that Rose was in the upper 50's. Now the people like Emily Young, John Ronches , I understand that they make more than that. We are not talking small salaries for these international folks. They make very good money off of our backs, and they dare tell us that they will not help us when we need them. Now this is the organization that we belong to. So my question to Rose, Emily, and John was is this a threat? If we do not merge with local 585 will we be outside the scope of help from any SEIU local and the international? And they said "yes". And that was the bottom line. Well I did not show it at the meeting but I was quite sad. Here we have our international big brother doing to us what they accuse the employers of doing to us. As the meeting came to a close, they asked who was in favor of the merger Nelson abstained, and I said flat out no and everyone else agreed at that time. As they were departing Rose said to me that by not agreeing to the merger, that I was acting just how the employer would have me do. I just looked at her. After they left we all agreed that the executive board should not make the decision, that we should let whole membership vote on it. I said they are bluffing. I never really heard Tom Kelly being sheepish, but he said to me in a quivering voice, "Harriet I don't think they are bluffing". Well needless to say, that was another personality incident that floored me. Tom was actually scared. I was swept off my feet. Tom scared. As a board we decided unanimously to take the vote to the membership. Billy contacted Rose and told her that was what the board wanted. It was not what Rose, and John wanted, but they did not want any publicity about it either. They wanted to keep this quiet. They did not want people on the outside to see how they were operating. The structure of local 29 was pretty unique. We were very much member oriented. We had to inform the members about everything, and that is the way it supposed to be. Now in 585 and other SEIU locals, it is basically the president who makes the decisions, then says to the members this is what you are going to get. There is not very much member input. So at the next general membership meeting, we as a board recommended that the members vote for the merger. I especially had to give a special report because I was in total opposition to the merger. I was asked why I was in favor of the merger all of a sudden. I stood and told the members that I was (not) in favor of the merger. But I recommended that we vote in favor of it because we were being (threatened) by the international. I told the members that if we went out on strike that we would have no help from any SEIU local or the international. I told them the plain truth. Our backs were against the wall. I did not tell the members that I thought the merger would be better for us as a local, I told them that it was better for us if we

31

wanted to survive in SEIU. So they knew where I was coming from. They had come here to take our local away from us, and they made it just about impossible for us to continue to operate in the way that we have been operating. I was very disappointed and I did not hide it. Well, it was disappointment and anger. They came in and just stripped us of everything. We were just starting to put everything back together. Why did they not take the local when George was president. I can answer that. It was easier to do what they did when there is an all black administration in control, than if there was a white one. It is much easier to get a negative response when minorities are in leadership. We cleaned up a lot of Detriech's mess. And none of that was taken into consideration. And one other thing that I was disappointed about was that I was planning on running for vice president against Dolores Barfield. Even though I loved being the recording secretary, I wanted to be a business agent. I loved working with the people on that level . It was a thankless job, but I would have loved it. And I might add that if I had run against Dolores, I (would) have won, easily.

The actual merger vote was at the union hall. When I got there to cast my vote, Billy was sitting in a chair at one of the tables. He was slouched down some and I walked over to him and I told him that I was casting my vote against the merger. Billy told me he voted no also. He told me that. He was very saddened by all this. He would have taken it better if he had been voted out of office. And there was a couple of people there from the international. John Listisen was with them. And he had bags from the liquor store!! The votes were going to be counted there. I believe most people knew that the merger was going to go through. John sure knew it. He was ready to get ripped. I felt so bad for Billy. But one thing, he did not put the blame where it was supposed to go. The international. We could have restructured without giving up our local. This was truly a crush to all of the sincere long time local 29 members. A lot of people (members) thought that things were going to get 'better'. Well this was just the beginning. The merger vote was won by a large margin. The votes were counted, John was getting sauced and it was just a glorious day (for some).

As I understood it, Rose had contracts with her business agents. They some what outlined their duties. They were not actually officers as was in local 29. Rose had to get her business agents for her building service division. First of all, Billy and Dolores were more or less forced into retirement. Billy would stay on a while longer as an executive vice president of local 585,but he had no power. He was stripped. There was nothing for Dolores. Rose had her eyes on Hermaine Delaney for a while as a business agent. She liked Hermaine. Hermaine knows her stuff. From what I understand she had her eyes on Rich Johnston as an organizer or business agent. Now remember, John Listisen was trying to get into the office too, since he was a part time organizer. Nelson was to be kept on as a business agent as well as Ed Zanath who was the lowest paid in the office. He was from the Detreich regime and Billy hired him (why he hired someone that was against him was beyond me.) When you have to play the diversity roll, at least hire someone that has the same ideals as you. Ed had a lot of complaints against him in the past. He was not a good business agent. Rose paid some special attention to me. I thought it was a good thing. I was hoping that she was going to offer me a job as a business agent. I wanted to be a business agent so very bad. Well, her attention towards me was not what I thought it was. I was talking to Billy at the office one day , and I told him I wanted Rose to pick me for a business agent. And Billy told me this, he said "Harriet, Rose would never pick anyone like you to be a business agent because she cannot control you". Billy said that to me. Now as far as our executive board was concerned, it was gone. 585 had their executive board and of course that was not going to change. So we decided that our former board would become an advisory board of building services to the president (Rose Trump). We had no power, we would just take the members concerns back and present them to Rose. That took everything out of the board. We were trying to keep local 29 in some way together but it just wasn't happening. After the first two advisory board meetings, everyone was so discouraged that it just fizzled away. We had no power whatsoever. Really, we were meeting for nothing. I was so heart broken. I will add that our last executive board meeting In July of 99 Rose came to , and she thanked us all for the encouragement that we gave to the members to merge with her local. She took us out for a late lunch, and we talked. She started to discuss the up coming SEIU 2000 convention that was being held here in Pittsburgh, plus the up coming Presidential election. She told us that our former officers would all be delegates and alternate delegates in the in the up coming convention.

Rose was a very good president in the administrative form. She knew very well that the merger was not as smooth as it seemed. She knew that there were lots of unhappy members. And she knew of two main ones, myself and Tom Kelly. She knew that we were both knowledgeable and very vocal. She wanted no problems. As a matter of fact she continued to pay the executive board wages just to appease us. It was requested that she continue to pay them until the end of the year. But she continued to pay them after that. I asked Billy about it and he said Rose and John Ronches knew that we were still getting paid. Hermaine said she was not cashing her check. But I cashed mine. Hermaine probably cashed hers too!!!!! Billy even said that Rose wanted (no) problems. It was as if she said anything to keep them as happy as they can be without creating a brouhaha. I give credit where it is due. Rose was a good president. A very good administrator. But she was not a people president. She was not interactive with the members. That was not her way. She had member all over the place, and all they knew was the name Rosemary Trump. I asked her could I be a business agent. First of all it took a lot for me to approach her and ask her. And her reply was "next you will want my job". Then she laughed. Well she was not really joking. That was a nice way of telling me no. I was not pleased with her reaction but I had to live with it! My focus was not her job, I truly wanted to be a business agent. So Rose had to have a person to run the building service division. A man by the name of Mike Salmon was sent in. he was paid by the international. His job was to be the Director of Building Services. He said that he was floating around from state to state, getting the buildings services in shape. He said he was from Wisconsin. He traveled a lot. He was a loud mouth guy. You know the kind that comes in and throws his weight around. Local 29 had a reputation of being hard to deal with. Mike came in pretty strong. But he got toned down after while by the members. Now like I said the business agents were supposed to Hermaine and Rich. Hermaine struggled with decision whether to leave Duquesne University as a member and become a business agent for Rose. She talked to me briefly about it. She had a cakewalk at Duquesne University, and she was not sure if she should give it up or not. Duquesne was in house and they had better benefits and higher wages than the downtown members. She always made sure that we knew that too. Duquesne was also a catholic university, so they had holidays and other time periods off that the downtown people did not have. That was a nice set-up over there for the cleaners. Like I said she had a cakewalk and she knew she did. She was not sure really what to do. Part of her decision was the fact that Rosemary liked her. And when Rosemary liked you, she took care of you. Well, Hermaine made her decision to become a business agent for local 585 division 29 building services. Even though the rumor was that Rich was going to be in the office the second business ended up being….John Listisen. When I heard that I was really shocked. I was told in the union office that John had got fired from the post gazette. I immediately asked Billy Joe about it. Billy was very vague about it. Billy represented him in case . He said John got fired for looking in some files and he was caught on camera. Billy said he could say no more. But something was not right to me. So I asked another person and that person said that John got himself fired so Rosemary would hire him into the office .And when John got fired that is exactly what Rosemary did. It took me a little while to figure out why Rich Johnston did not like John. He told me he did not care for him (most people did not) but Rich was the kind of guy that got along with everyone. Well, that was supposed to be the reason why. It made sense to me. John was making 15 dollars an hour cleaning. It was apparent that his boss let him have his way in union activities on company time. Plus John had 10 years there(at least that is what he said). And all of a sudden he got fired for something like that? But like I said Billy would not tell me much of anything. But all the pieces fit into place. John was ready to take over Billy's former office and was quite excited about it. But John always said he did not want to be hired as a business agent. He wanted to be an organizer. At least that is what he would say. When I talked to my mentor (Nelson) about it he just chuckled. I asked Nelson one evening that he was riding me home from a meeting, how could he get himself fired when he supposed know the ins and outs of that building??? The timing was impeccable. Billy was not saying much, now that part kind of threw me. Why was John's case/ settlement so hush, hush? Especially from Billy?? We have always talked about other cases in depth, why was this one so special??? Well this is how it ended up, Rose wanted Hermaine so she was in. Rich was supposed to be in, but John got fired and he ended up in. So it was Hermaine and John. Now I must not forget Ed Zanath. He was put by Rosemary as some type of agent between the healthcare division, and building services. From personal experience, Ed was totally useless. And Nelson was kept on as a business agent.

Now, since Mike Salmon was hired to be the director of division 29 building services, the members were trying to get use to him ,plus all the other changes. The members demanded Rosemary, but she was not a "local 29 president". Rose made all the big decisions, but she was not going to become a people president. She was the administrator. The head honcho. She had the people in place to do what had to be done, but she had the final say. I believe the last membership meeting she came to, she tried to get the members all pumped up, but it wasn't happening. One female member said that if she kept ranting and raving like that she was going to have a heart attack! Tom Kelly was so upset about the merger. He did not like it at all. At the membership meetings he was still himself very, very vocal.

Meanwhile, preparations were being made for the up coming SEIU convention. This was to be a huge event. We had a meeting at the 585 office with Woody Gibbs, and he made it clear that Rose wanted us to be a part of this convention. And he specifically said "Rose asked for the members of the advisory board". He was waiting for a response but I just couldn't dredge up the 'I feel special' mood. As far as I was concerned, we were still local 29. (only in my head!!!!) The convention was very big. There was gold and purple everywhere. Our public transportation, the Port Authority of Allegheny County had special buses to move the people around the city. I tip my hat to the drivers, (Mr. Larry F. Thomas), Lenny Porter, J.J. Jefferson, Fleetwood Taylor, Miss Joleen, Butter, Jimmy Pearson, Bill Coleman, and all of the other Port Authority drivers that helped make the convention a success. I did get to meet some out of town members. I was in class with a lot of them too. Mike was very upset that most of the members chosen to participate in the union seminars did not show up. He was very upset. He had a number of tables reserved and most of the members did not show up. I was a little dismayed too, but you have to keep in mind the mindset of most people in general. They just want everything to be all right. There was even a private concert for the members at the Civic Arena (now called the Mellon Arena). Patty Labell was performing. Also at the close out of the convention, of course President Bill Clinton was present. And of course the Reverend Jesse Jackson was also present. The building that I worked at was right across the street from the convention center, but I did not attend the two most exciting events (to me). That was the President Clinton and Reverend Jackson. I was an alternate delegate, but I would have gotten too much hassle from my boss to get paid for the day. After the convention was all a thing of the past, there was a retirement party for Billy Joe and Delores. It was held at dowels in downtown Pittsburgh. It was a very nice affair and Billy Joe deserved it. There were a lot of people there. It was very nice. I personally hated to see him have to be forced down like that. Billy truly believed in the union the way it was then. Working for and serving the members. He truly had a heart for that.

Now that all of the festivities were out of the way, it was back to business. Tom Kelly was on Mike's back. He and Mike Salmon did not hit it off at all. He was becoming a thorn in Mike's side. In June of 1999, Tom Kelly resigned from the advisory board. Even though Tom was the way he was, he was good to have around. He kind of kept you on your toes. I don't think that anyone noticed that Tom was really a threat to Mike Salmon but Mike Salmon. When Mike would mention that he had lots of friends at the international Tom would cringe. Mike did mention that frequently. Tom talked of CMU decertifying . Mike told me that if Tom started that ,that he would make sure that "Tom Kelly would not be able to join any other union again". Now those are powerful words. Tom always said nothing could be worse than local 29. Well, at one point he retracted that statement. He said "I thought that nothing could be worse than local 29. I was wrong". Tom never participated in the conferences that local 29 had. He thought going to other parts of the state and or country for conventions etc. was a waste of the member's money. He was a trustee and he was on the list to go. But he did not want to.

Mike was starting to get into the groove of things. I would visit the union office a lot. Since we were local 585 now things had changed. I had to deal with the representatives of 585. I would talk to Levon Livingston ,who was a business agent and official of local 585 on a regular basis. Hermaine told me to watch out for him. I was a little shocked that she had said that. She never said why. To me Levon was more her type to be under than mine. I would talk to Woody Gibbs occasionally. Woody and Levon were buddies. Woody's wife's name is Harriet! I thought that I might add that.!!! Tom Hoffman did not like either one. Woody came from the post gazette. He was hired by Jack Yoedt during his presidency as an organizer, but he never got a chance to do his thing because Jack was voted out. He was later hired by Rosemary. But I had to deal with Levon and Woody on non building services issues. Only things that involved campaign issues and conferences etc. now back to Mike, I had to try and learn him. I had to see what he was about. So as I said I visited him often. It was getting close to contract time for the downtown buildings. Mike knew that I was on the negotiating committee. Mike sent out surveys to all of the members to get an idea as to what was the most important to the members. The survey issues were numbered from 1-10. Wages and healthcare are always the main issues. Grievance handling should not be on there. That is what they are supposed to do. (That contract is a legal document and the officials are to uphold it. It is illegal for them not to.) So anyway the negotiating team was in place. A guy named Jay (I forgot his last name) was sent from the international to back Mike up on the negotiations. Jay was a negotiator. He was making sure that Mike was doing things the way he was supposed to. He seemed to be a friendly person. I guess I kind of compare everyone to John Ronches!!! So everything was going good at the round table. Or I thought. Mike seemed to be buying into the friendliness of the CPS. I could see right through them but Mike was all in it. He would refer to cps as being "our friend". That did not set right with me or other committee members either. Well, little did we know what was going on behind our backs until it came to cps violating the contract. The building that I worked at was about to relocate. Not shut down, but relocate. The city of Pittsburgh wanted the space to expand the Convention Center. Well there was talk of us the cleaning people were not going to the new building. I brought up the situation to Mike Salmon. I told him that it was not a "new building opening" it was the relocation of the old building. The old building did not shut down, it just had to relocate. My boss was going to try and not carry us over to the new building, but it did not work. A letter to the owners and my company was not very pleased with it. But we were concerned for our jobs. So after all was said and done, we went over to the new building in September of 2000. Meanwhile my boss, Mike Salmon, and John Listisen were all getting very friendly. Mike referred to my boss as his "polish friend." He would laugh after saying it, but I did not think that it was funny.

Coming up soon was election time for local 585 officials. Rosemary never had any serious challenges in the past. She had been president for 25+ years. She did build that local. There was a guy challenging her this time named Jim Neville. I had never heard of him and neither did anyone else I asked. I was asking Hermaine about him and she got a little defensive. I did not know why. She said she knew nothing about him, but she understood that Jim Roddey the head of the Allegheny County Council encouraged him to run. They were both republican. Jim Neville worked for the county in the clerical department I was told. He had his people with him who were going to run for executive offices too. Personally I blew it off as just a person trying to unseat Rosemary. Little did know that the 585 officials were very nervous. I do not remember Rosemary campaigning very much. I guess she felt that she did not have to. Well, I was one of the ones chosen to count the votes. I guess there were about fifteen people or so. Don't forget, local 585 had members in a few different places. The ballots were sealed. When I got to the local 585 office, there was a strange atmosphere there. There were constables there armed, there was something going on there that I was not aware of. I saw Rosemary and I greeted her. It was strange because she was always so bubbly and happy to see her people, but she was not like that this day. Everyone was tense or it seemed to me. I saw Levon but was his usual self . I knew something was wrong but I had no idea what it was. As were seated by the officials at specific tables, I still had no clue what was going on. At local 29 we never did vote counting like this. Armed guards and so on. But I understood why the ballots were sealed, because they were mailed in. Rosemary had out of state members too. Everyone was seated at the table that they were assigned to. Each table got lots of unopened envelopes and separate boxes in which they were to be placed, according to the person and the position being voted on. We had an instructor who was telling us exactly what to do. As I started opening the ballots, I was a little startled at first. There were quite a bit of votes for Jim Neville. But I thought that it would slow up. Well it did not. Not only was I starting to become a little worried, it was coming to me why all of the tension and the strange mood Rosemary was in. for her to be feeling this way before the election, she had to have some type of feeling that this was going to be very close. As I had understood in the past, other people had run against Rosemary, but never came close. Apparently the staff knew that it was going to be a close battle. And the huge difference between this election and the others was that local 29 was now local 585 and we had a lot of voting power. At the end of the voting, Rosemary Trump had lost by over 200 votes. That is a lot in this situation. She lost convincingly. The atmosphere there was so, so thick you could cut it with a knife. After we were released from our counting I went out into the hall. John Listisen was not very happy. And he definitely was not getting sauced, at least not at that time. He may have afterwards but it was not a celebration sauced! I went to look for Hermaine. She was sitting on the floor in tears so upset and mad and she was just mumbling about how thing did not go right. I did not understand what she was talking about . There were the 585 officers around her comforting her. I went off to find Levon Livingston in his office. Well he was trying to be himself, but it was not working. I finally got a glimpse of this guy Jim Neville. He was dressed to the teeth. As I remember he and all of his people won.

Now the stuff starts to hit the fan. Rosemary Trump filed charges against Jim Neville. The charges were election misconduct, illegal loans, nepotism, violation of democratic principals on the part of Jim Neville and vice president Dennis King and Eric Wolfe. The meeting was held at the former Doubletree Hotel across from the city of Pittsburgh convention center. There were a lot of people there and certain people were asked to speak at the meeting. I was one of those people. Mike Salmon coached me as I am sure they did the others. We wanted the local to go into trusteeship and then we would end up having a new election for president and Mike Salmon would be the front runner. Also when I got to the meeting I told mike that I really needed to talk to him about the violations of the contract that were taking place at the building that we had just relocated to. Mike said to me that he did not have time for that now, and what did he want me to do about it. Well needless to say I was quit upset with his attitude. After I spoke my piece at the hearings he actually hugged me and kissed me on the cheek. No, I did not feel good after that. I was still very upset. But anyway as the hearings went on, I did not know how to feel about the outcome. They tried to play the race card against Jim Neville. I had heard nothing about that until evening. That stuck in my mind. They said that Jim Neville wanted everyone to stand and salute him at the board meetings. Frankly I thought that was kind of funny!!! But I still always where this guy Jim Neville came from. The way I saw it was that (someone) had to guide him into path to take this big step to run against Rosemary. Hermaine told me at the office on the election day that "everyone thinks that the international likes Rosemary but they really don't". And I will say that I simply did not believe Hermaine. (I) knew that the international liked Rosemary. There was nothing that pointed to otherwise. Rosemary built that local. She was the president for 30 years. She was an executive vice president of the international union. She was known. Her name carried power. She was strong. If she liked you, you were liked. She would take care of you. No, in my mind Hermaine did not know what she was talking about. She was just talking off the top of her head. Well, towards the end of the hearings Mike said to John Listisen as I listened, "Rosemary will never get it back." So to me that meant we were going to have to have another election after we get out of trusteeship. So after the hearings, I left with Levon Livingston to head for home. He was not optimistic. But he was so cheerful all the time it made you feel a little better.

Several weeks later, Mike Salmon called the division 29 advisory board to a special meeting at the union office. Mike was telling us that it was all over for Rosemary. There was no way they were going to turn the election over and give her the victory. Mike said "Rosemary fucked up". She did not campaign hardly at all and that she was riding on her name and reputation. She really did not think that she could be unseated by this Jim Neville. Well when I got to the 585 office to count the votes, Rosemary was not herself. So for Mike to say that she thought that she could not be unseated, she sure was not showing that at the election. I know what I saw. She looked extremely worried. So Mike went on to tell us that he wanted to be the next president of local 585. His heart was in it and he loved working in building service. He made it clear that he wanted and needed our support to become the next president of local 585. He said that if it happened with our help that he would be very partial to our wants and needs. He said that some people would recognize that but he did not care. Like I said Mike came here from Wisconsin. He sold his house there because he thought that he had a permanent job here. He wanted to stay here. Now keep in mind that Mike was not very well liked by a lot of the members. And he was very friendly with cps and other management folks. But for now he was running building services. But the Jim Neville situation was still in progress, and so was our local going into trusteeship. Now Jim Neville ended up out of office(mysteriously). We were appointed a trustee from out of state. I never really knew her name. She was at a local conference that we had on the south side. She spoke for a while but nothing was really said. To me it was more or less a type of rally for the shop stewards. There were some SEIU representatives there from New York. Mike Salmon and Tom Hoffman were there. There were also some members from the university of Pittsburgh. I was surprised because the university of Pittsburgh members rarely went to things as such as far as I had been going. Or course the conference was all about organizing. Now don't get me wrong, organizing is very important, but SEIU is legally bound to uphold that contract. It is a legal document. I left the conference early with Mattie Faye Hines. I was not interested in organizing when the contractor I worked for was being(illegally) allowed to violate our contract by Service Employees International Union Local 585.

Several weeks after the conference, the trustee that was appointed to us went to take on another SEIU job in another state. She was no longer our trustee. So who ends up being in control as deputy trustee, none other than Tom Hoffman. There was an article in the newspaper about Jim Neville filing federal charges against Service Employees International Union. He claimed that he was wrongfully relieved from his "elected office". At a membership meeting at the union hall, a gentleman from Rose's 585 asked Tom Hoffman about the situation with Jim Neville and where it stood. Tom Hoffman blew him off and everything was under control. He gave no information about it at all. I never heard anything else about Jim Neville or the lawsuit. I would ask around at the union office but no one knew nothing. Jim Neville just seemed to vanish into thin air. I was approached by several members and asked was he paid off, but I said I had no idea of that. But it made me think. If this man illegally used our union money, then we should know all of the details of the union's dealings with him. But, we were told nothing. Nothing at all.

So it was back to the usual with Mike Salmon. I was really battling with him and John Listisen. When we moved to the new bank property, my boss really started going crazy. I am speaking of the director of operations for cps. My one supervisor Mike D'Angelo said I left a bag of trash in the hall. It was a lie. Cps was asked where the trash was left. The write-up said it was left in the hall. Then it was said it was left in a department. I said what department, they said they did not know. I work daylight and every morning myself and co-workers had to remove trash left by the male night crew. So I documented the incidents. I went to the city of Pittsburgh Human Relations and filed discrimination charges against my employer cps. The first thing the intake officer asked me was what was SEIU doing about it. And I simply said "nothing, that is why I am here". I had proven it was a lie. At my grievance meeting Ed the director was there, Mike was not there and John Listisen the business agent was there and he sided with Ed. Cps lied in the write up had no proof of their lie and John Listisen said I had to go to counseling. As we were leaving the meeting my boss Ed Garzcewski the director operations for CPS said to John my business agent, "don't forget you work for me". John turned around and laughed and said "no I don't." Ed walked

45

away and John told me that I would probably have to go to counseling. I said what!!! I was appalled. I contacted Mike but he sided with John and......Ed. Hermaine Delaney was in on the case also. She was right on the money. She said the write up was ludicrous. Anyway I was licked. John told me, well it is only a verbal so it really does not matter. Now that is my business agent telling me that. It may have been a verbal but it was a lie. And when John found out that I filed charges at the city of Pittsburgh, he was not pleased. He said to me that he wish I had not done that. Debbie Watson who was Mike D'Angelo's assistant was now at my site permanently. When I would come in in the mornings, Debbie would try to talk to me. She had gripes about the little money she was making. I did not have much to say because I am not a morning person. She commented on my jewelry and I thanked her, but I did not have much to say. If there was a special assignment then I would accept it and walk away. So when it became vacation time we the veterans picked our vacations as we always did. Well, she would send the picks back denied with no reason. So I filed a grievance. And the grievance was according to the contract. We have a grievance meeting. John comes and Hermaine was with him. I was glad to see her because she is a good business agent. John said he asked her to come because I did not trust him. He was right. I made no bones about it. Well, we went by the contract. John sat there with his mouth shut as Hermaine did all the talking. At the end of the meeting, John said nothing and Hermaine said that the grievance needs to go to arbitration. As my boss Ed and John and Hermaine were getting off of the elevator Ed was very upset and he said to John that he was going to call Mike Salmon about this grievance. A couple of days later I get a letter from John that the grievance was going to arbitration. I was very glad. I knew that CPS was going to lose. It was clear by the contract. About a week and a half later, I got a call from John to come to a meeting at the union office. When I got to the office Ed Zanath was there with Mike and John. Hermaine was not there in the room. Ed Zanath told me that the grievance was not going to arbitration. I became very upset. Mike Salmon left the room went into his office and shut the door. I was left with John and Ed. Ed said he did not think it should be challenged and that the company was right. I turned to John gave him some words. He had the gall to jump out of his seat as if he was going to attack me. I just looked at him. He knew better than to step to me. I said what I had to say then I left. I was so upset. Our union (Service Employees International Union local 585 –29) was blatantly allowing the contractor to violate our contract. Local 29 after the Jack Yoedt administration was not like that. So I got all of my papers together and went to the National Labor Relations Board. I filed charges that our contract was not being upheld. I do not and will not take frivolous grievances to the office to suggest that they go to arbitration. I am known not to do that and I have gotten flack from my members at times about that. But this needed to be challenged. What was happening was that cps was trying to strip the veterans of our contractual seniority earnings. Well, like I told the members, that type of behavior is expected from the employer. What the members were now seeing was that our union was not going to uphold the contract. Our union was not going to fight for us. My co-workers were not seeing things as they were, because they just wanted everything to be made right. Meanwhile, I am very upset. The contractor is blatantly violating our contract, and SEIU local 585 top officials are allowing them to do it. That is illegal. The contract is a legal binding document. For the company to violate it is illegal, and for the union not to uphold it is illegal. So I got all of paperwork together and went to the National Labor Relations Board. The intake officer said that there have never been so many complaints against local 29 until this merger with 585. She said that to me. So I gave her a verbal summary of what had happened. A few weeks later an officer from the department was assigned to my case. I took my contract and the all of the other proper papers that I needed. She read the grievance and the contract and said to me, "why would he (John) not challenge this". I told her that rumors was that he was doing favors for the contractor. She said she was going to investigate the case. She seemed to be very surprised that the grievance was not being fought. She by what she read that John Listisen was a "poor business agent". I reread my notes that she took and I was satisfied. She then told me that she would be starting an investigation and she would be in touch with me. By her attitude I was kind of optimistic. So it was out of my hands. I waited impatiently for weeks for an update. Well several weeks later, I did not get an update I got a ruling. That ruling was "just because SEIU did not take a case to arbitration that I thought they should have does not mean they are in violation of anything'. I was so very upset. I filed the same charges with the NLRB in Washington D.C. and they told me just about the same thing. We have a past practice clause in our contract. That clause was ignored by the contractor. I filed the grievance and SEIU said they were not going to fight it, and the NLRB agreed with SEIU. And just for the record, the person who handles the case does not make the decision on anything about the case. The regional director does. So I was upset. But John was happy. He and Mike Salmon. If that case had gone to arbitration, cps would have lost. So this entire situation was really frustrating me. Here we belong to this union, SEIU. We pay union dues every month . These officials make very hefty salaries off of our dues. Let me say that I have no problem with that. But when our union is going to help the contractor falsely reprimand (and eventually lead to termination) union workers and refuse to legally uphold our contract, then I have a huge problem with that. And the National Labor Relations Board is supposed to correct that. I then called a few people from other buildings and they gave me similar scenarios. I was learning that former members with 7 years and more were being terminated. I would ask about members and I was told that they had gotten fired. It was becoming clear to me that this was becoming a pattern. And I had to ask myself why and who would benefit. This situation did not come to my attention until we relocated to the new building and the oust of Billy Joe Jordan. But I will say this, I do not think that Rosemary Trump would have ever let this mess go on. I believe that she would have fought grievances. That is probably why she is no longer the president. Hermaine Delaney said that "people think that the international likes Rosemary , but they don't." I will never forget Hermaine said that. I said to myself at the time that she was just talking trash. The international loved Rosemary. So now I have all this stuff going on in my head. I had no one to trust. Nelson was gone. He had a tragedy in his family and he retired. They tried to get rid of him, but he was not going to let Hoffman and company get away with it. But after the things that went on in his family he decided to let it go. It was the best thing for his family. I understood that. But Nelson kept up with a case he had out at Carlow College. I truly missed my mentor. Back to the situation at my building, my supervisor Debbie Watson was as best that I can say 'out to get me'. After the SEIU let cps violate our contract about the vacations, Debbie was still on the warpath. She was obsessed with our locker room. She said our locker room never passed inspection because it was not tidy. And she did not want cartoons etc. on our lockers. She also did not want us to keep anything on top of the lockers. This supposedly went for the men's room also. We had tables in our room and she said that we could not leave anything on the tables. It was so ridiculous. So I would check the men's locker room, and they had stuff on top of the lockers and stuff on their tables. So things were beginning to get clearer for me. I got the daylight male co-workers to witness the 'violations' of their locker room. The stuff that was left was from the night crew. Debbie worked at night. Debbie made such a big fuss about the ladies locker room. We also have a 3-11 shift. Carolyn Chapman works the second shift. She is a whiner and a trouble starter. She always tried to create friction with the females on daylight. At first I thought she was ok. Then when I experienced the things she was trying to do against me and my co-worker Niki. I stopped talking with her and just greeted her. I also may add that she was friends with the supervisor Debbie Watson. As I was saying Debbie was making a big deal out of the ladies locker room. One night she cleaned it. Keep in mind that Debbie was management. I had a magazine on the table .It was on the second shelf of the table. When I came in the next morning it was gone. She threw my magazine away. So instead of approaching her, I called the General Manager of CPS. I told him what had happened. He told me he would speak with Debbie. Well, when I came in the following morning, I was given a written reprimand. Debbie had Mike Bannon another supervisor with her. I started to read the paper, and I start shaking my head. I got half way through the letter and I said to Debbie "give me a pen". I had to sign it or I would have been sent home. I signed it and put "signed under protest". I handed her the sheet back. I looked at Mike and he gave me a sincere look back and shrugged his shoulders. They both left the locker room and I started to get dressed in my uniform. I made my cup of coffee and sat down and started to read the write-up. I read it once. I am not a morning person. I read it again. I could not believe it. I have duties in the main 24 hour department in the bank. I do the same thing every day. I know the people and they know me. The manager knows me. The supervisors also. There are 3 shifts in this department. I know the twilight supervisor, and the midnight supervisor. We all relocated together. I did the same at the old location. Vacuum and empty trash. Trash that is tagged and dated. This is a very busy department and it shows. It needs special attention and it got it. I work the 7-3 shift. 7am-3pm. My other duties were another department which was not 24 hours, but time sensitive, and was only cleaned on daylight early. That was me. I also had kitchen and cafeteria duties. My daylight boss Chad Manzer was in and out daily. When complaints from departments, they were addressed. They would split the duties between us on daylight. There are 4 cleaners and 2 utility men. I did not attend the restrooms, but they were the most important subjects in the building. So when complaints came in, I was given the bulk of the duties. The management office would call Chad and Chad would come and rearrange the duties. We did not mark them on our list of duties because they would change. I was to end my day in my department. Well when the cafeteria was reporting numerous calls to the office there had to be a change. The trash was overflowing continuously. So Chad was called and he split the duties among us all on daylight. I had the last kitchen and cafeteria run. I was specifically told that that was where I was to 'end my day'. I asked what about my normal schedule and I was told that that has changed. So, I did what I was told. Chad did not inform Debbie. Daylight functions were priority. That is when all the big shots are there. The building manager was also in on the decision and change of my duties. The write-up stated that I did not perform my duties in this department the previous day. The write-up also stated that I had been told about leaving trash in the departments. So it was becoming clear to me that cps was trying to build a case against me that would eventually lead to termination. I had to calm myself down and plan my next move. I could not call the union office just yet, so I held off on that. It was apparent to me (and others) that John Listisen was working with cps. The write-up said that a supervisor from that department said that I had not cleaned in there. I must add that the write-up was timed for 9:30 PM. Now remember, I work 7am-3pm. It stated that none of my duties had been done. Since the write-up said a supervisor (bank supervisor) reported me, then I wanted to know exactly who this supervisor was. The manager of the department said that she knew that I cleaned in there, and if she wanted me to call the building manager she would. She also stated that her twilight supervisor was off, and she was not going to have cps lying on her people. I asked her not to call the building manager, but to call the general manager of cps, and I gave her Lou's number and extention. And I remember her words "I will not have your people lying on my supervisors". When I went to clean the building manager's office, I told him about the situation. He told me "that's impossible. They must be playing with you". So I left it at that with him. My next step was the city of Pittsburgh Human Relations Department. I all ready had the discrimination charges against them. So I went down to put these charges on them too. They were harassing me. So I gave them a copy of the write-up , the names of the bank manager . Then the officer asked me again, "what is SEIU doing about this"? and I said "helping cps"!!!! He just shook his head. I needed a statement from any witnesses that I performed my duties. After I got home from the city-county building, I started to write my general manager a letter with a copy of my write-up. I bypassed Ed the director of operations because he was in on this. And there was another cps supervisor's name on my write-up. A Jeff Taylor. I heard of him but I did not know him. I did not even know what he looked like. But in his letter to the union, he witnessed that I did not fulfill my duties. So in my letter to Lou I told him that the bank manager of the department would be contacting him. And I also put in the letter that she said she would not have his supervisors lying on her people. I filed a grievance (demanding) that this bogus write-up be taken off of my record. So, I had to be in touch with John because he was the business agent at that time. Debbie Watson and cps had the gall to write a total lie on me and basically say there is nothing you can do about it. And how....because cps knew that SEIU 585 was not going to fight it. And all this time I am thinking there is someone missing in this whole picture. Now, by me filing the harassment charges with my discrimination charges, the charges take an additional spin. The city of Pittsburgh was going to have to interview (every) person in that department including the manager to see if I was there performing my cleaning duties. So in between the time of my grievance meeting I received a phone call from a person that had a written statement for me. I received the statement but I did not inform anyone except the city of Pittsburgh because they had to have it for my file for the interview process of the department employees. Well, I made 25 copies of that written statement. As I said I told no one. I did not even tell MR. Bill a co-worker who was the night time shop steward. I did not trust him with certain things. This was a serious matter, and I backed off from telling him. But I wanted to so bad. So the time came for my grievance meeting. John came but much to my surprise Hermaine Delaney was with him. John said he wanted Hermaine with him(again) because I did not trust him. Well he was absolutely right. I don't trust John. The meeting started and my supervisor Debbie started off with "Harriet don't like me". John had his tablet out. I don't know what he was writing. Probably nothing. Hermaine then said "what does that have to do with anything"? John was not saying anything. No surprise there. Anyway I was going back and forth in the meeting, and then my boss Ed then tries to get tough with me. Ed thinks he is the Al Capone of contractors. Anyway my meeting was at a close. Ed wanted to have a recess with Debbie. Well, just as they were about to leave the room, I said oh, I have this sworn statement that I did my duties. I thought Ed was going to die. He said what? I had so many copies, I just started passing them out! John was not happy. Hermaine was herself. Ed said why did you not tell me you had this. I said because I did not have to until now. He said well you should have told me sooner. And I said no I should not have. I said to him that I filed this amendment with the city of Pittsburgh, and they will be interviewing everyone in that department, not only the person that signed the statement. Well, cps did not want (anything) like that to surface because the bank would see the forged documents and Ed would have to answer to all of the lies that he and his supervisor created. Cps would have lost the contract with the bank. So I was ready. Ed went out for his recess. As we were sitting in the office, John was sitting there looking at the statement. He said "you did not tell me you had this". I said I know. He then said to me that I should watch the person that works 3-11 because she was involved. So that was Carolyn Chapman. I was glad John told me that because I always had in the back of my mind that she was involved. I turned to Mr. Bill who was the night steward and said to him "I knew that she was involved". Ed and his supervisors came back in and Ed said that the write-up would still stand. I said fine and that I would see him and his crew, the bank employees and John at the hearing the city would have after their investigation. I got up and was walking to the elevators. Ed followed me and Mr. Bill out. I looked at Mr.Bill and I said "I can't wait for this". Ed then pulled out his cell phone and began to call someone. John came out of the room and got on the elevator with me and Mr. Bill. John said "Harriet I don't know what Ed is doing, but this was supposed to be removed from your record". So now you can see the relationship that Ed and John have. I told John "I have no problem with his decision". I went back to my duties and Mr. Bill went home. Mr. Bill later said "you sure made them all look like fools when you gave them the sworn statement." So I was fine. But there was one person I had to meet up with and that was Carolyn. Carolyn has a lot of issues. She has a problem telling the truth, she is not very attractive, and she is very , very jealous. So when I am about to leave she is coming in. I waited for her in the room where we have our time clock. She came in to hit her card. I greeted her and I said to her "I had a grievance meeting and guess whose name came up"? She said who? And I said yours. The first thing that came out of her mouth was "Harriet I did not try to get you fired". She went on to say "they are lying on me, they are lying on me". Now, listen to the next events. Carolyn ran to the guard's station. She called Debbie Watson and asked why she was mentioned at the meeting, and that she did not want to be involved. She also said that I was going to physically abuse her and that she was scared.(I was on my way out of the building and to the bus stop.) Debbie then called Ed and Ed called John. So later I got home. Later that night while I was sleep , the phone rang. It was John Listisen. He said he was calling me from his cell phone. He was (very) upset. He said that (my) boss Ed called him earlier and cursed him out for telling me that Carolyn was involved in that situation. He said that I was not supposed to say anything to her about it. (John is telling me this.) He said that Ed really jumped down his throat about it. I said to John "so". He said oh, you don't care? And I said no. He said ok and hung up the phone. Now why would my boss have a relationship with my business agent like that? John did not and was not going to fight for me at that meeting. John knew that the entire thing was a way to build a case against me. Hermaine told me on the bus that John was so very upset that I did not let him know that I had the sworn statements. He was upset because he was not able to tell Ed about them. Like my boss said to John that day "don't forget you work for me". A few days later, I received a letter in the mail from cps stating that the write-up was removed from my file. The reason given was the time 9:pm. And my boss also stated in a nasty way that the next time I have a written statement to produce it earlier than I did. But I know that I don't have to do that. One thing about these contractors you have to be on your toes, because SEIU will not fight for you. So John was very upset. But such is life. And I ask the question, why would he be upset? Well, when me and my co workers were talking about it, they said John did not get paid from cps cause he lost the case!!! And I told them, we laugh but it ain't funny. I was trying to make my co-workers see what was going on. CPS (dare) present me with a severe write-up and (dare) tell me that I did not do my assignment for that day. Debbie Watson (stuck) that piece of paper in my face and told me, this what I can do to you. I had a department full of people that witnessed me doing my work. The only way she could have had that (confidence) is if she knew she had backing from the SEIU. Billy Joe Jordan would have never let that case get that far, and neither would Rosemary Trump. If I had not fought this case on my own, it would have stayed on my record, and I probably would have been fired. Don't forget, the write-up said that a (supervisor) said I did not complete my duties. That is grounds for a transfer or dismissal. I worked at the bank for 23 years, and SEIU was going to allow them to steal my livelihood from me. I believe they have done it to others no doubt. And those people need to come forward. And I am not talking about members who abuse their membership. People that do things and then run to the union and say 'save me". Or the ones that think they cannot be fired because they are in a union. I am not talking about those kinds of people. I was and still am appalled at what SEIU is doing. So, my case was done. Debbie really hated me after that. And John was not pleased at all with me at all either. So what?

Several weeks later, one of my co-workers showed me a letter that he had received in the mail. It was addressed to him, and it said that SEIU local 585 was planning to take the building service members out and put us in a local up in Ohio. It stated that it was being done to strip us of our voting power. The letter was short typed and anonymous. I made a copy of it and posted it on our bulletin board. Rocco my co worker asked what did I think about it. I told him that it sounded true. There was talk of building service going to an out of state local. And the two locals in mind were in Detroit and Ohio. Now the part about the voting power was for the most part on the money. The former Local 29 rocked. We had mega voting power. When Rosemary was voted out, the 585 people blamed the local 29 members. There was a hot issue with that. The 585 members were very upset for a long time. They said we were the reason why. Everyone was trying to figure out where this letter came from. I called Hermaine and she said the letter was not true. But I knew better because the talk of us being shifted to another local was being talked about. But as I understood it this letter came from Mike Salmon. Tom Hoffman was not very pleased about it either. Mike really wanted to be president here. But that is not what the international had in mind. Mike always claimed that he had many friends at the international. I wonder where they were at that time. I had not been to the union office at all. I could stand going there being lied to all the time. I hated calling John. It was useless. But I had to keep in touch with him because he was our business agent. I would see Hermaine on the bus quite frequently. I would speak with her about the stuff that was going on. I continually would tell her about John and his relationship with cps. And she did say to me one time that if it is true that John was playing both sides, then she could understand it because he had to look out for himself if he was fired by the union. Well, this was just so foreign coming from Hermaine. Hermaine was a straight up union fighter, or I should say used to be. She told me at one time that she wished she had stayed at Duquesne University as a worker. Every time I would see her on the bus, I would complain about cps and John. Hermaine also tried to get information from me. She was asking me about the letter that was sent to members about the voting rights and locals in Ohio. I told her I did not get a letter, but what the letter was true. And she tried to say that some of the letter was not true. I think the whole thing was they were trying to find out where the source was because the letter was (true). And they knew it. I saw and read the letter. It was true. Later on I understood that Mike Salmon was leaving. I tried to get information why , but I could not get it from John or Hermaine. All I kept hearing was rumors. Now remember, Mike came here from Wisconsin. He was working for the international. He was working under Rosemary Trump who everyone who worked for her felt very comfortable. And I can understand why. Rose took care of the people who worked for her. I remember when we went to the SEIU convention in Washington DC right after the merger. Rose took all of the SEIU persons who attended the conference out to dinner. It was an expensive restaurant. She told us to order anything we wanted. Well I got a lobster tail and mashed potatoes. It was good too!!! I asked Rosemary was she related to "the Donald Trump". She laughed and said no!! But anyway there were at least 30 of us there. Hermaine did not go because she stayed at the hotel to attend the workshop for the African Americans. She did not like the fact the Rosemary had the dinner at the same time as that particular workshop. And then Nelson went but he did not eat. He went back to the hotel. So I was with Billy Joe. He was still very hurt about the merger (and rightfully so). So yes Rosemary took care of her people. I really wanted to get the scoop on Mike Salmon. All I got was that Mike was leaving and was very bitter. I was told that he was being accused of writing that anonymous letter and that he was not claiming that. I was also told that he was no longer being considered to be president of local 585. Now after rosemary was gone, Mike had to deal with none other than Tom Hoffman. He was the deputy trustee. The big question was how do break up local 29 and the local 29 mindset? Hermaine even said that they do not know what to do with yall (local 29 members). Local 29 was a fighting union. We fought the employer. We had to. The contractors constantly violate the written agreement. Other locals in SEIU do not do that . Billy Joe told me that Andy Stern told him that his main problem was fighting grievances. Now listen at that. He was telling Billy ,if you had not fought so hard for the members you may still be in there. Now this is the SEIU International President for the "working families union" saying this. Don't fight for the people. I will address that later on.

After Mike Salmon left a gentleman named Adam Kushner was chosen to be the director for division 29 building services. He was with Rosemary and local 585, but I do not know what title he held there. When I called the office and asked about him, I was told by Nelson that he seemed to be a fair guy. I was told to not be hesitant to tell him what was going on. Well I took the advice. Later on at my site we had a grievance come up about the (utility) classification. Now listen closely again at what was about to happen. The PNC properties have a utility classification. This job requires a lot of heavy lifting, and a lot of heavy furniture moving, and it also requires delivering packages (to all the different departments in that particular building) from light to extremely heavy. It pays 2 dollars more an hour, and it should. It takes muscle to do that job. We have two utility guys at our site. Cps wanted the job eliminated and contracted out. But due to heavy security reasons, the bank said no. Our people were trusted. All the employees knew us. Now when the utility guys are off, another co-worker usually takes their place and gets the higher wage. A few times some of the other female workers would fill in because of the higher wage rate. The only female that filled in and did all that the job required was Peggy Przybilinski. She did it all. She no longer works with us. I really miss her. Now when Evelyn took the job a couple of times, she could not do the job properly because she did not know how to work the power lifts and could not lift the heavy boxes, etc. I told her that if she could not do the job that she should not sign up for it. And the few times Niki did it, she was forced to do it , but she did only what she could. I never signed for the job, because I knew I could not do what the job required. Now before we moved to the new building, my two big bosses came to see our utility guys and try to scare the one into retiring and the other (Rocco) into taking a guard job somewhere else. At that time Mike was still the director. As soon as I had learned that my two bosses had been there, I yelled at them (the utility guys) for not calling me to the meeting. (They were scared!). I asked them what did Lou and Ed want and they told me that they were trying to make them leave so the utility position would not be carried over to the new building. After I learned what had happened I immediately called Mike Salmon and left him a message on his vms. Later on that day after I got off, I went to the union office and talked to Mike about it. Mike said he talked to Ed and told him not to be going to the sites and trying to scare the members. He said that Ed said that we are his employees also. Mike also told me that as long as PNC wanted that job in place it was not going to be eliminated. So when we went to the new building, Rocco and I went first. Rocco was doing utility and I was doing the cleaning. Everything was so out of place and the building was not even finished so we were all working together to get everything in order. Several weeks later Niki came over. Now she had to help do the utility work because I have more seniority than her and I did not want to do it. That job you can easily get hurt on and it puts a lot of strain on your body. As a matter of fact, Rocco had a dislocated shoulder and was on light duty because he was doing that utility work by himself when we first moved to the new building. And over at our old building Rocco was off then on light duty for a long while because he had a pinched nerve in his shoulder from that job. He also had a broken toe from an accident with the heavy equipment. When Niki came over and she had to do the utility work she was not pleased at all. But she gave it her best shot. Her and I was at the freight elevator on day and all of our big bosses were in the hall and Niki is very hyper. She yelled at Ed my boss and said was she going to get the utility wages because she has to do their work my boss Ed said "if you are doing utility work, you will get utility wages". And I told her "I told you". Because she had been asking me was she going to get the rate, and I told her yes. Now there were many cps supervisors in and out of the new building. One supervisor told me that Ed went to the real estate department and asked if he could contract out the utility work and the bank said "no". The employees knew us and there would be no security risk. So learning of this, and I got that information by accident, I was not concerned with the threat of the job being eliminated. The work was there and the guys were working it. And whoever filled in when one of the guys were off, got the higher wage. So eventually all of the veterans from the old building were at the new building. My self, Niki, Rich Evelyn, Mr. Bill, Laurie (we were the cleaners) and Art and Rocco(the utility guys). Mr. Bill and Laurie were still on the night shift. The rest of us were on daylight. Everything was going as usual. When one of the utility guys was off rich would fill in and get the higher rate. There was one incident where Rich took it upon himself to help the utility men and he did not get authorization from management. He left a note on his time card that he had helped them and that he should get the higher pay. In response to his note to Debbie, she told him that 'he was not getting the utility rate because what he took upon himself to do was not authorized, and not to do that anymore'. I have a copy of the note as I have copies of lots of other notes and documents. So Rich told me about the incident and I told him that Debbie was right. I told him that he could not do that. So I told him there was no need to fill out a grievance because he was wrong, and if he did file a grievance that I was not going to sign it. I was very adamant about that. If the contract was being violated, then I will be on it. But if a member would come to me with some oki-doke mess, I would let them know I was not going to sign my name on it. They would have to go to Mr. Bill who was the night shop steward. Several weeks later one of the utility guys was off. Instead of Rich replacing him, someone from night shift was ordered to stay over and do the job. Rich remained on his regular duties. Well, Rich was very upset at this and he went to get the contract. Rich stated that by the contract he was entitled to work the vacation because he had more seniority than the person that was selected. I did not even have to read the contract. I told him that he was wrong. I told him if John and SEIU had not let cps illegally take our past practice rights away, he would be justified in his argument. He was going by contract language that was referring to vacancies due to a retirement or termination. I told him he had no case. Then Art the senior guy said oh no a vacancy is a vacancy. I said no. I told him that that person was on vacation, so the job is not vacant. They can get anyone they want to fill in for vacations. Well they were both very adamant about it. When someone goes on vacation, it does not have to be posted. So what I did was I went to a neutral person the dock guard Larry. He got brains. I asked him about the grievance. I gave him the situation. Larry said that what I was trying to tell them was correct. There was no defense for that grievance. None. I told him if our past practice rights were not gone , he would have a solid case. But he filled out the grievance anyway. One thing that I could not understand was what would make him think that John would fight something that was not contractual. He did not even fight the stuff that was!!! Well anyway Rich went to Mr. Bill. He put his name on it. But needless to say the grievance went nowhere. Now Rich was upset with me because I did not sign it. He was acting like a little baby. Art was a little upset too.(Frankly I did not really care because I did not deal with them personally) But minus the past practice, the contract did not address the replacement for vacation issue, and it never did. So after the grievance was turned down it was business as usual. So the next time a utility person was off, Ed said it was ok for Rich to fill in because he (was not) going to pay him utility wages. So Rich filled in and guess what? That's right he did not get paid (even to this day). I talked to Ed and his reason was that there was (never) a utility position at the new building. So I went to Rich and had him fill out the sheet. I submitted the grievance. It was denied by Ed on the grounds that Mike Salmon had made a (secret deal) with cps to eliminate the position. Now the position is there and being worked every day. So I went through the motions with John. John also said that Mike said the job was gone. I told him that made no difference. John was trying very hard to make me drop this case. He calls me with Mr. Bill on the three way calling. He continues to say how Mike Salmon was to blame for this. Of course I was not buying it ,and Mr. Bill was not saying much. John went on to say that "Ed is never going to win this in arbitration". And I could not believe that he actually said that. On a three way call at that. So I did not say anything. John went on to help Ed by saying that Ed had been over paying us and no one inquired about it. I told him yes I did and I had a letter that I had written to payroll about that. John was so shocked. He said "you do"? I said yes. He was so surprised. John decided to end the call so he hung up. I could not wait either. When me and Mr. Bill's lines were clear, I asked Mr. Bill "did you hear him say that Ed would never win the utility case in arbitration?" Mr. Bill said "yes I heard him." Now I ask why would our SEIU union official know this and help the contractor? And why would John bring up an issue about the overpayment to try to make me back off the case? And how would he know about the overpayment anyway? And why would he (our SEIU official) threaten to use it against members? So of course he sided with Ed. Well, I was so upset. I called Tom Hoffmann. After I made three separate calls to him he decided to call me back. The message was on my machine. Meanwhile I was in the process of writing to International President Andy Stern. I told him what was going on and that we wanted John removed from our site. I also told him of the grievance problems that we were having. I sad to him if we did not get this matter resolved that we were going to go public with all of this illegal mess. Well I got no response from Andy stern. So I got all my papers together to go to the National Labor Relations Board. I had serious reservations about it but I knew I had to go. I knew I had to have everything in order to present the case. I must add that the petition I got together to have John removed, Rich would not sign it. He was upset that I was not backing his previous grievance. I guess he really wanted me to make a fool out of myself for him. That was not happening. I went to the National Labor Relations board. The lawyer that I was assigned to seem to be very fair and smart. Well, she was smart. I presented her with all of my paperwork plus a copy of the contract that was pertaining to the issue. She was taking the notes as I was talking. I assured her that everything that I was saying was the truth. Not only that, I had the documents to back up everything that I was saying. I told her that I had reservations about coming back there. I asked her if the board ever ruled in favor of any situation like this to her knowledge. She said no. I asked what was the purpose for it's existence . She made reference to strike purposes, but (none) where the local was held accountable for illegal actions like what was being presented. After she took my report, and read it back to me I asked her what she thought of the allegations. She hesitated and she said to me "they (local 585) have a lot of explaining to do". She told me she was going to start her investigation. She said that if Mike salmon worked as a federal mediator that she would have to get Mike Healy (the attorney for local 585) to get in touch with him. But I asked her what Mike Salmon had to with the fact he cannot illegally violate the contract. He was gone. So I calmed myself down and thanked her and left. I actually had the nerve to be somewhat optimistic about this situation. I had (everything) in place. I had all the documents. And before I go any further I would like to add a very important situation. The letter that Debbie Watson wrote to Rich Pavicic was in his possession from the start. At the beginning of all this, I asked him if he had it because I remember him showing it to me after she gave it to him. I asked him to make me a couple of copies because I needed them and he did. Well before I went to the labor board, I could not find the copies he made for me. I knew I had them but I did not know where I had put them at home or in my bag. Now Rich like art keeps a copy of everything. When I was making the case for the labor board I was frantic cause I could not find this note. I went to Rich and he said he would get it out of his locker. Well, he comes back to me and tells me that he cannot find it. He went through all his stuff in his locker and it was not there. He told me it was probably at home in his stuff. So I am frantic. This letter was extremely important. So he said that he had no idea where it was. I was very upset. So I figured that I just had to go to the labor board without it. I went home and I was going through my bag to make room for everything I had to take to the labor board. When I was unfolding papers that I had thrown in my bag ..there was the copies of the letter. They were folded and in between the copy of my contract that was folded over. I was elated. But I always had in the back of my mind that I could not believe that Rich lost that note. He had it for so long in his papers and it was very important. But he had everything in his folder except (that). So what I did was I made many copies of the note from Debbie. And when I went to work I did not tell Rich tat I had found the copies. (After) I had gone to the board, Rich told me he had located the note from Debbie. I told him at that time that I did not need it. He said he found it at home in some papers. Now why would he do that? These men were so 'oh well" about all this stuff that was effecting all of our lives. When Billy Joe who is black was the president everyone was pulling out the stops to have him removed. I believe Rich wanted me to fail. He just happened to come up with note after I went to the board. I knew that the investigation would take some time. At least twelve weeks. Well in less than eight weeks I believe, I had a call on my answering machine from call the labor board. I did not have any ill feelings, I was just a little surprised at the time it took to get back to me after this so-called big investigation. Well I called the attorney that had my case. She said to me that that the investigation was over and that they were just going to "call it lack of

65

evidence." At that point I just lost it. I started to yell at her. I asked how she could call this as such. She apologized and said that she was just the middle person and that she did not make the decision. She apologized again and I hung up. Several days later I received a letter stating that there was lack of evidence for my case. And that Mike Salmon and SEIU had some how eliminated the job. I was so upset that I did not know what to do. So I wrote to Arlen Specter and told him of the illegal conduct going on in our local. I got nothing positive from him. And I had not heard from John either. The last time the labor board rejected my case he had the nerve to send separate copies to each member . The members were not pleased with that either. So I decided to seek legal help outside the local. I went to Paul Goltz Legal Services. I made an appointment. I had all of my papers with me. I presented my case to the gentleman that I was told to see. After he got all of my information he went to Mr. Goltz . I was a little nervous because I did not want to hear that there was no grounds for a case. So I waited and when he came back he said that I had three avenues.1, arbitration, 2 go to the labor board, 3 hire an attorney. I told him that the union was not going to go to arbitration, and that I had been to the National Labor Relations Board, and they said I had no evidence. I told him that I wanted to proceed with the legal services. He told me that the office would be in touch with me soon. I said fine. I told the members that we would want to do a class action case, and that we could all pitch in pay the costs. I tried to make it very clear to them what was happening here. We are paying a lot of money in dues. Which no one minds if our officials are doing their job. But they are not. They are letting the contractors violate our contract and they are agreeing with it. That is illegal. Contracts are written agreements with signatures on them agreeing to abide by it. We could be fired for nothing and the local would not do anything. I tried to make the members see this. Especially the veterans. Several weeks later an attorney , a labor attorney named Martin Clancy called me. I was getting a little anxious, and I quickly had to calm myself down due to the fact that everything else failed. So I wanted to make it clear that I wanted it to be a class action suit. He asked me to begin with what was going on. And he did let me know that he knew Mike Healy the attorney for SEIU local 585. I figured that he did because there are not many labor attorneys around, and plus attorneys know attorneys! I told him briefly of the first situation but I wanted to focus on the last grievance which was the elimination of the job classification. I began telling him about the utility classification and the cleaning classification. He asked me what the job involved and I told him the differences. I also had to tell him of the fact that the local is blaming the elimination on Mike Salmon who is no longer an official for SEIU. I told him that Mike had quit and was now a federal mediator in Wisconsin. I told him that the lady that had my case at the labor board would had to have Mike Healy contact Mike Salmon and get a statement from him stating that he made a secret deal. Mr. Clancy was taken aback. He said "they are not allowed to do that". He asked me if the job was still being worked, and I told him yes. I told him that SEIU was not fighting this at all. He asked me why and all I could tell him was that the rumor going on was that John was apparently helping cps and possibly other contractors. But by the union meetings that I attended, SEIU was not addressing this problem . I was brushed off at these meetings. The more I told Martin Clancy the more he laughed. And I don't mean he laughed in a funny way, he laughed in a disappointing way. I was picturing him shaking his head while he chuckled. After I gave all of the specifics, I told him I wanted his opinion of whether we had a case or not. He said we most certainly did. So I told him that I wanted to think of everything that I should tell him along with other questions and he said fine, and for me to get back to him. Well, I was pretty optimistic about this. I went back to work and I told certain co-workers that we may be moving forward in this situation. But for the most part, I remained silent on the matter. My main questions were payment for Mr. Clancy and what we wanted from the lawsuit. Several days later I called Mr. Clancy. I got his answering machine and I asked him to return my call. And he did.....about a half an hour later. I told him I know that he was going to ask me what results we wanted. He said yes. I told him that we wanted we wanted that position restored and if there were any damages that we wanted that too. He told me that there would be no damages due to the nature of the case. He also told me that litigation was very expensive and that he did have to put bread on the table. But we still have a case. And I asked him if SEIU could be liable for the legal fees. He said they could. And I also asked him wouldn't the exposure of this case be beneficial to him. There was no response to that. So after that ,inside of me my heart sunk again. He said that he would be back in touch with me because he wanted to check into a few things about this case. So I said ok. Well, I had not heard from Mr. Clancy for a couple of weeks. I called him again and he asked where I lived and I told him. He told me he was in Plum and he said that we could get together and go over our current contract and all of the papers I had. He said that he would get back to me. So I was a little optimistic again. Well, Mr. Clancy never got back to me. I wanted to give him room because when there is no money up front I know you have to be patient. I waited and I waited. No call from Mr. Clancy. A few (months) later I called Mr. Clancy and left a message on his machine. I asked him if he was still interested in the case to get back to me and I left him times to call me. Several days later he returned my call. He had not talked to me in a while and he asked me to refresh his memory about what we had discussed about the case. And I did. He gave me the story that even though we had a case that it would take a while. And he asked me about the national labor relations board. I told him (again) that they had refused the case and the reason why they did. His entire attitude was different. He said that there was not much that we could do since the national labor relations board turned the case down. He said that we could go to court but judges don't like cases like that cause they take a while. His entire attitude was I don't want to be bothered with this. He was trying to discourage me. I was thinking in my head after I hung up that he was not in touch with me because he thought that I would let things go. So after that disappointment, I had nowhere else to turn really. I was so disappointed and frustrated. It took me a while to tell my co-workers.

The next monthly union meeting I went to, I was approached by John Listisen. He told me that he was no longer the business agent for my site and that Hermaine Delaney was the business agent there now, and that he hoped that I was happy. I was surprised to say the least. There was no memo or notification of any kind. And I was happy. So when I saw Hermaine at the meeting I approached her. I told her that I just had found out that she was our new business agent and that I was glad. And her response was that she was not there to "clean up any of John's messes". So not only was I thrown by her response, I was not surprised. I said to myself that that was par for SEIU local 585. At the meeting we find out that we have a new director of building services.(I was told that Adam was forced into retirement by the local). His name is Gabe Morgan. A young guy from Chicago I think. As far as I was concerned they were all the same to me. They were just out to keep (their jobs). Upholding the contract was no longer an issue. Just organizing and keeping the union dues coming in was their focus. So there was a major campaigning action beginning here. Since I was not on the inside anymore all I could do was go by what I was seeing from the outside. And it was not pretty! When I would go to the union meetings, the issues of the contract being violated was not an issue. All Gabe would lie and say that their so many loop holes in the contract. That was a lie. And he and the rest of the officials knew it.

Right before John had been kicked out from our site, there was a grievance about the raise that my boss had been giving us for several months. This was a non-contractual raise. At the time that particular money was added to our wages, we had gotten our next to the last raise which was 30 cents an hour. About two weeks after that raise another 40 cents was included to our hourly rate. I thought this was not right. I know my boss Ed and he does not make mistakes like that. We were not allowed to call our employer about payroll issues at that time so I did not call. Plus I was dealing with payroll concerning my AFLAC insurance deductions. The lady in payroll that was handling the union payroll personally was a lady named Shannon. Before that it was another lady who's name I forgot. And before it was a guy named Kent, and so on. When I would go to lunch I would call Shannon and ask her about my payroll deductions. Most of the time she was on the phone or out of the office. So when I did get to her, we set up a way for us to be able to contact each other. I would send her my questions via inner office mail. And she would leave the answer on my answering machine at home. It worked out good. It was not an on going thing , it was just at the time where I had to get all of my payroll deductions correct. So while I was asking why my AFLAC deductions had stopped, I also asked Shannon about the extra 40 cents an hour in my hourly wages. Like I said earlier, I felt uneasy about that. CPS don't make mistakes like that. Payroll just can't add money to a person's wages without authorization. So I said to myself, let me check with my co-workers. So I asked two of my co workers Niki and Rich did they get extra money in their paychecks. They said they did not think so. And I asked them don't they look at their pay stubs? And they said if they were over paid that that was their fault. So no one got back to me on it. So automatically I thought that it was Ed that had that done just to me. So what I did was when I was inquiring about my AFLAC insurance with Shannon, I asked her if the extra 40 cents per hour was correct in my pay check. In fact I told her what my pay rate was and that I believed that the extra money was a mistake. I wrote this in a brief letter to her. And when I got home her answer was on the machine. She told me there was no mistake in the extra money that was added on to my regular raise. Well I was satisfied with that. I got the ok from payroll. But my co-workers had lied to me. They knew they were getting more money. If I had known that , I would have dug into it much more than I did. Well, this money was being given for several month which added up into hundreds of dollars per person. My boss Ed came down unexpectedly and told me that he wanted to have a meeting about the repayment of the mistake that was made by payroll. And before I go on with this situation I must make this point. Before John was taken out of our building I had a grievance meeting with him Ed and a co-worker. At the end of that meeting John said to me "I will get Ed to admit that the management was notified of the wage increase. In the room at that time was myself, John and my co worker Evelyn Patterson. I slightly shook my head in agreement with John. I was not impressed by his 'we are going to get them' attitude because I know John was just playing games. He and my boss try and put on this 'we don't like each other relationship', but they are so transparent it ain't even funny. So when my boss came back into the room, John mentioned to him about the fact that I contacted payroll about the increase. Ed said "yes she contacted payroll, but she should have contacted me". So I was at least glad that Evelyn was there to witness that. Now back to the meeting, Ed came down and Hermaine Delaney was with him. Ed pulls out a calculator and starts to go through all of this stuff. I am already disgusted but everyone else is sitting there just taking this mess. No one is speaking up to tell him that he is wrong. He says that the utility guys were overpaid for many years. They were getting paid on a percentage. We were not. So anyway my boss made up this payback scale. I left the meeting before it was over. I was called back after my boss had left. Hermaine was taking the notes at the meeting . So she said that the cleaners owed several hundred dollars and that the utility men owed more. My co-worker art said that my bosses pay scale was wrong and that she should go back and get the contracts that show that they were paid on a percentage. Hermaine said that she was not going to do that. (Why) would our SEIU business agent refuse to get the information from the union office to prove the contractor wrong? The information is there. Why did she refuse to do what she was supposed to do? So she said that my boss was going to withhold our next pay raise. So we filed a grievance. Hermaine gets back to me and says "Mike Healy says he can't do that". My boss told Hermaine to tell us that if we go ahead with the grievance and we loose that he was going to take all "his" money back in one lump sum. Hermaine told us that Mike Healy(the attorney for SEIU 585) said that "we did not have a chance in hell of winning that in arbitration". So we were all scared so we took the advice not to go to arbitration and to let the boss return our contractual raise back in the next contract along with whatever we raise would bargain for. So the payback was set at a little over four hundred dollars for us all. But my boss took over one thousand dollars off the utility guys. We filed another grievance on that. Hermaine wrote me a memo stating that the pay back was correct. That was a blatant lie. I have all of the documents. Why would she agree with the company? They were dead wrong and she knew it. Yet she agreed with them. During the course of one of our meetings with just Hermaine , I mentioned the issue of the utility position being illegally eliminated. It sparked her interest. I gave her a brief summary on the issue, and she said that there was nothing that had happened to eliminate that job. And I told her that John helped cps eliminate it. She said "John has done a lot of stuff". The only thing about Hermaine was that one day she would tell the truth about John then the next day she would defend him. So I told her that we were going to resubmit the grievance about the utility elimination issue. Well we file it. Later on we had a meeting with my boss and the utility crew. My boss said that the grievance had been resolved. I said that it was not because everything that went down was illegal. He told Hermaine "Harriet just wants this to go to arbitration". And I said that is correct, because if you say that this position is gone legally, then I am sure the arbitrator will see it that way too. Well, my boss was not very pleased at that meeting. Several days later I get a letter from Hermaine stating that the grievance would go on, but cps was going to file charges against SEIU local 585 due to the fact that the union at that time said the issue was resolved . So I told Hermaine that we still wanted to go through wit it. I did not care if cps filed charges against SEIU. If they had done right by the contract it would have never come to that. So I waited and waited. A few weeks later I called Hermaine and she told me that she had to talk to Mike Healy about this grievance and that he was not available. He was out of town due to family issues. A couple of weeks later I get a letter from Hermaine stating that it was the position of SEIU to uphold the previous decision on that particular grievance. It was written by her and signed by her. So that was truly the end of that. I was very upset. I even had to ask myself (what did you expect Harriet?). Hermaine has not been in touch with me sense I received that memo from her.

I keep in touch with Billy Joe Jordan. I was telling him about the stuff that was going on. He was truly heartbroken. He told me earlier about the taking back of the money grievance, he said "Harriet don't let them take your money. Ed tried that when I was in office and I stopped it". And when Billy said that to me his voice was so sad. He could not believe that this blatant behavior by union officials was being allowed. I told him that I did everything I could to stop it but SEIU is on the company's side. Billy would have never ever let this stuff happen. Rosemary either. I should have gone to Joe Pass like Billy told me to when I told him we were looking for a lawyer. But our options are still open. I will never go back to the National Labor Relations Board. I truly believe that the National Labor Relations Board is the government's way of getting back at people that belong to unions! They are totally useless.

The downtown buildings contract was about to be up. SEIU was staging rallies and meetings to I guess pump the members up. Well the actual pumping up was just plain lying to the members. At the meetings they were trying to make the people afraid so they would vote for a strike. I would stand up at these meetings and tell the people that they were being lied to. I questioned Gabe and Tom's motives about their tactics. Some of the officials were not pleased with me but I did not care. They wanted members to go out on streets stop traffic and get arrested. SEIU took out a full page add that the contractor Quality Services was discriminating against African American workers. That is mostly who they hire. Me and a guy from another building were talking about that. The articles that they had in the paper just did not add up to me or the guy I was talking to. The guy had told me how the contractor he works for was treating the workers bad and John was siding with employer. I told him that this sounded like Tom and Gabe playing the race card. Now they are both white. I could not believe that Quality Services was letting them get away with that sham. SEIU local 585 wanted to give the impression that they care about their African American workers. At one meeting Gabe was trying to make the members believe that if they went out on strike they could come back into the buildings making astronomical amounts of money. They tried to compare our situation with Boston. They told lies about how all this stuff happened in Boston and that they won a huge contract for all of their workers. Well, a worker from another building gave me clips from the Boston Herald about the SEIU janitors strike. As I was reading this, I just started shaking my head. I went on line and went to the

Boston archives to get the full news on the strike. By the time the news got to me and I was able to get the truth, the meetings to raise union dues (a lot) and to yet merge again with an out of town SEIU local was over. Still, at the next meeting I saw Rich Johnston (the arrest guy) and I showed him the copies I had gotten from the Boston herald. He said to me "where did you get this". I told him on line. What was printed in the Boston herald and what Gabe and Tom were telling everyone were two different things. I gave the articles to a couple of members but they never got back to me. So as the contract negotiations got closer SEIU was trying different tactics to make the members scared. When I talked to Hermaine, I said to her that she knows that I have been on the negotiating committee and I wanted to remain. She said that she knew and that I was definitely going to be on it. I even signed up for it earlier just for the record. Rich Johnston was contacting me for a little while and he was discussing the plan for a possible strike. I was totally against it. I told him like I told Gabe , how are you going to make or try and make people strike in a recession? And he told me that we could make it work. I told him on no uncertain terms that I am not going to lie to these people. If they walk off the job they will not be back in this building. What the SEIU officials were doing was pitting the new workers against the veteran workers. Of course the veteran workers made top wage. So that was one of the SEIU tactics-to keep the new workers mad at the older workers. The new workers said that if they made what we made that they would do all of their work!! And the union was supporting that mindset. They said that if all the members went out to rally that we would get what we want, which is much higher wages and (full) hospitalization for every family. I would tell the people at my building, do you actually believe that? I would tell them to read the paper, look at the economy, look at what people are losing everything every day, and you are going to let these people tell you that going out into the street and yelling and screaming and stopping traffic is going to made these building owners give you whatever you want? I told them SEIU is yelling strike but they have not even began to bargain yet. And I also told the people at my building that SEIU officials are allowing the contractor cps to violate our contract. All they could see was that we the veteran member deserved it. And that is what the union wanted as well as the cps contractor. Well, when the negotiating committee was formed , guess who was not on it? That's right, Harriet. I must admit I was very disappointed. They kept me off it. A young lady named Jannie Marshman was put on the committee. She believed in what SEIU was saying but when she approached me I would give her the truth and let the chips fall where they may. Jannie is a good girl and I respect her. I thought that she would be all right . You have to let people see the truth and then make their own assessments. The SEIU officials would continually beat into the non senior members heads that if they wanted a "good contract" that they needed more people out there to rally. They were keeping the tension going on between the two classes. When Rich Johnston called me we talked briefly and I told him that I was against a strike. He went on to tell me that we were going to lose everything if we did not strike. He told me that I had to be on the same page with the local . I told him , not when the local is wrong. So Rich stopped contacting me. The rumors that were being spread were against the senior members. The rumors included that our wages were going to be cut in half. I called the office to talk to Hermaine . She said that our wages were not going to be cut, and that they were just trying to scare us. I did not repeat that to anyone because she would have gotten into trouble at the time. So I decided to take a different approach. I contacted the Pittsburgh Post Gazette. I told the writer for the paper the things that were going on in our local . The scare tactics and misrepresentation of SEIU. The reporter told me that he had a meeting scheduled with the big wigs of local 585. I told him that he must have been talking about

Gabe and Tom Hoffman. The following week, I contacted the paper to see how the meeting went. He said (Tom) was asked about the situation. I was told that Tom was very shocked at the questions and he denied them. A couple of days later I saw Jannie. She works at night so I caught her in the morning. I asked her what was going on in negotiations. She told me that Gabe told all the committee that they were not allowed to tell the members what was going on because someone went to the Post Gazette and told them a bunch of lies. I did not tell Jannie that I was the one that contacted the Post, but I am sure that Tom knew because he knew what was told to the reporter was (most true.) I will not give Jannie's response. I told Jannie to look at what was going on. When I was on the negotiating team as far back as Jack Yoedt, we had to take notes and report back to the members at our site. We (had) to tell them what was going on. I knew it was not her fault. But I asked her to think about this… how am I going to negotiate your livelihood and tell you that I cannot give you a progress report because the director says that I can't. That is crazy. But SEIU did it. I told my co-workers to call tom Hoffmann and (demand) that they be told what was going on. One girl called and she said she got a recording. She said she thought it was strange because that had never happened before. So I don't know if tom Hoffmann was going to put out a report with the post gazette before I called, but later on he put out an article with the Tribune Review (the other local newspaper in town). The article was very interesting. The only thing was that most members did not even realize what was being said. And I asked my co-workers did they read the article and they were not really interested. Briefly the article stated that wages were not the issue. Hospitalization was. But SEIU knew that it was a national problem and that they just wanted to bring attention to "their" efforts with rallies and demonstrations. And I will make note again that in that article (interview) with Tom Hoffmann, it stated (clearly) that the very popular "Justice for Janitors" slogan was started in "Denver then quickly got to Pittsburgh". That is a (lie). That "Justice for Janitors" started right here in Pittsburgh Pennsylvania by Billy Joe Jordan in the 1985 SEIU lockout of the downtown building cleaners. Now I am curious as to how Denver got into that article. It was a total lie. Did Tom Hoffmann who really disliked Billy Joe have had it printed up like that? Did the Trib make a mistake and get Pittsburgh mixed up with Denver? And why wasn't the mistake corrected? Or was it a mistake? And why was the interview done with the newspaper that most people don't buy? Earlier in the weeks before negotiations started was a rally at a church in downtown Pittsburgh. The fliers said to bring your families , families deserve a living wage and family coverage hospitalization. Well SEIU got together with the pastor of the church to have this fiasco. That is what I considered it. You know tell a bunch of hard working people to come to a church, and let it be known who is sponsoring it (SEIU) , have food (which they did) and have the pastor pray. Well I will say this without apology and with (divine) comfort and assurance, you (cannot) manipulate JESUS CHRIST. It was just another ploy to make the people think that SEIU cares about them. And sad to say, a lot of the members were going along with it.

At the end, there was an extension on the downtown buildings contract. A week extension. A lot of members were scared, but at my site members that wanted to cross the picket line would have been able to do so with protection. This entire scheme to strike was concocted by SEIU. It was not about protecting the working families. It was about bringing attention to service employees international union, to make people want to join the union, and keep the dues coming in to pay the hefty salaries of the officials. It also plays a huge part in politics. Most of the time, members that vote for who SEIU tells them to vote for. They pour lots of money into campaigns. Personally I do my own homework on candidates. But don't get me wrong, all of that plays a part in the union industry, and I understand that. it is the way that things are run that I will not agree with. And I am not alone by a long shot. Gabe Morgan talked how the former local 29(then 585 division 29, now local 3/29) was the backbone of the building service divisions across the country. He went on to say that to remain there we had to merge with the local from Ohio to remain strong. I stood and asked Gabe if Pittsburgh is so much the backbone of it all(and local 29 was) then why don't local 3 come here and become part of us? He then said that I was being sentimental about the entire thing. He never gave us an answer. Do you know why? The entire plan was to bust up local 29. We had a lot of voting power and they had to break that up. When a president did not do his job he was voted out. Hermaine even told me that they had to stop that. All of this stuff that mike salmon, Gabe Morgan, and Tom Hoffman have done and are still doing would not be going on if we were local 29 or 585. Now we belong to a out of state local and we don't even know our officials. I do not even know the president's name. And most of the members don't. SEIU tells us that these mergers are being done all across the country. I would like to know how many African Americans and Hispanics have power positions in SEIU? And I am not talking about organizers. I am talking about presidents and vice presidents, etc.

To successfully change the original mindset that the union belongs to the members and that the members have a final say-so in the matters, you have to try and get rid of the old heads that know that that is the way it supposed to be. You have to shut them up. Stripping us of our voting power was the foundation of SEIU's plan. Ever since that had been done (finally with ousting of Rosemary Trump), SEIU has been eating us up. Andy Stern (SEIU International President) told former president Billy Joe Jordan, that his problem was that he fought too many grievances. When the contractors violate the contract, that is what has to be done. Now, when we file a grievance we are told that management is right.

Even though the opposite is written in the contract. Members are disciplined for acts they did not commit. When a grievance is filed. Nothing. The officials pick and choose who they are going to fight for and how hard. When that contract is being violated, it is illegal for SEIU not to uphold it. Not only is the employer performing an illegal act the union is too. Yet SEIU mocks the members, laughs in our face as John Listisen does, and tells us that there is nothing we can do about it. Then the labor board agrees with the illegal acts. I can say that if we were able to find a lawyer to fight our case it would have made a difference. Not only members from my building, but other buildings too, are saying and asking, why are we in this union? SEIU is in with management. We may as well not file a grievance, nothing happens. They are taking our money and not fighting for us. When are we going to have another membership meeting? All of the feedback I get, I tell them that it is not about us anymore, it is about them (the union officials). That is why I wrote this book. I wrote it to bring attention to what is really happening in the "working families union" SEIU. I want to let other members around the country know that this is not the way it is supposed to be. And I want other members to know that if the same things that are happening to us are happening to them that it is illegal. Class action lawsuits are encouraged. I believe that people that apply for such jobs in the cleaning industry should have a choice whether to join SEIU or not. Maybe politicians should introduce laws concerning "closed shops". And there should be laws set by politicians that would allow members to withhold dues when the "union" violates the contract. That's right when the union violates it. When they don't uphold it they are in violation. I also believe that their needs to be a serious overhaul of the National Labor Relations Board. They need to be accountable to another government agency, like the Department of Labor or even the Justice Department. When they allow the laws to be broken they need to stand accountable. Isn't that the American way?

In closing, I would like to say that the commercial cleaning industry is not easy. A lot of people think that we just go to work, clean a certain area and that is it. Well it is not like that. (we wish that it were). It is a cut throat industry among the contractors, and all the heat falls back on the workers. The contractors under bid each other for cleaning contracts and they know that the work cannot be performed yet they dump it upon the workers. The senior workers are forced to do their assignments and assignments left by workers who don't care whether they get fired or not, and we better do it or we will get fired. There is a clause that speaks to that issue in our contract but we cannot file a grievance on it because SEIU will not honor it. The supervisors are rude and ignorant. Some of them are drunks and come to work in that state. All of that falls back on us. And not only do we have to fight that , we have to fight our union(SEIU) also. That is the sad part. I will always remember Nelson's five famous words, "what does the contract say"? To SEIU it means nothing . And we actually pay for this (disservice.) And (SEIU) has the gall to label themselves as the "working families union". Yeah, we work for the SEIU official's families. Maybe if we were able to select unions like we do car insurance, SEIU would do what they are legally bound to do.

About the Author

Harriet Jackson was born and raised in Pittsburgh, PA. In June of 1980 at the age of 20, she began working at one of the major banks in town, in the housekeeping dept. There she joined S.E.I.U. Local 29. Several years later she went on to become appointed shop steward and contract negotiator committee member, and recording secretary and executive member for local 29. Today she is in her 24th year at the same site and is a member in good standing of S.E.I.U. local 3.

www.ingramcontent.com/pod-product-compliance
Lightning Source LLC
Chambersburg PA
CBHW020340290526
45785CB00005B/2108